FIGHTER TEST PILOT

From Hurricane to Tornado

ROLAND BEAMONT

Patrick Stephens

Frontispiece *With full reheat, the TSR2 begins its take-off run.*

First published in 1986
First paperback edition 1987

British Library Cataloguing in Publication Data

Beamont, Roland
    Fighter test pilot : from Hurricane to Tornado. — 2nd ed.
    1. Beamont, Roland   2. Air pilots — England —
    Biography   3. Air planes — Flight testing
    I. Title
    629.134'53'092   TL540.B/

    ISBN 1-85260—064—0

Printed at The Bath Press, Avon

*Patrick Stephens Limited is part of the
Thorsons Publishing Group, Wellingborough,
Northamptonshire, NN8 2RQ, England*

10 9 8 7 6 5 4 3 2

FIGHTER TEST PILOT

Contents

Dedication

To the ground crews and engineers of RAF Fighter Command, and the servicing and airworthiness teams at the factories, who kept this pilot flying safely for more than thirty years.

Disclaimer

The opinions expressed in the following chapters are the author's own and do not necessarily reflect those of any other authority referred to in the text.

Introduction

The years 1939–79 were momentous in aviation for they saw the final eclipse of the biplane by the monoplane; the first major war dominated by air power; the evolution of the gas turbine 'jet' engine and of swept-wing aerodynamics which led to practical supersonic flight; and, at the end of the period, the revolution in navigation accuracy brought about by the successful introduction of inertia and other advanced navigation systems.

This period also encompassed the author's time in aviation which included flying and testing experience of over 160 different types and variants of aircraft ranging from the beautiful open-cockpit biplanes of the 1930s to the supersonic auto-terrain-following Tornado of the NATO air forces in the 1980s. Each one of these was a fascination. Some were sheer pleasure to fly and others inevitably less so; and one of the greatest satisfactions in test flying was the ultimate achievement of excellent flying qualities in aircraft which had at first flight revealed poor, or sometimes dangerous, characteristics.

Of all these different aircraft, 49 types were test-flown at the factories or in Service operational trials, and nine jet types were evaluated at test-centres in the United States. Out of all this came the clear conclusion that despite the revolution in computer technology in the 1960s, '70s and '80s, the role of and vital need for the qualitative judgement of the experienced test pilot remains of paramount importance in the development of new aircraft.

In all this activity the author flew the first-flight and early test programmes on four major new military prototypes, sixteen new-type variants and many hundreds of new-build aircraft off the Hawker, Gloster, English Electric and British Aircraft Corporation production lines; and this enthralling experience led to a number of conclusions, among them that the British aircraft industry has produced many of the world's finest designs and still has this remarkable potential for world leadership but is continually inhibited in achievement by vacillating government policies on defence procurement. So often incoming governments have cancelled firm programmes placed by their predecessors after heavy R&D expenditure and before the RAF has been able to receive their badly needed new equipment — and the taxpayer has paid in any case and for nothing.

It is for this reason that the English Electric Lightning, which was first flown in 1957, still remains in service in 1986 as the only all-British supersonic aircraft in the RAF; no British replacement ever having been procured. Though coming to the end of its much extended 'useful life' it is still a supreme example of the handling qualities required for a supersonic fighter, and of the ability of British industry to lead the world in this field. At First Flight the Lightning was at least ten years ahead of world technology, and in the next ten years of Lightning development testing the author experienced more sheer exhilaration and enjoyment from it than from any other aircraft.

The following pages describe some aspects and incidents in the development and proving of a number of famous British aircraft, and some not so famous. All gave the author enormous satisfaction to work on and contributed to a feeling at the end of forty years of flying that the British can build the best aircraft in the world given the chance; and that all things considered it was almost a shame to take the money!

R.P. Beamont

Bibliography

The following sources of information are gratefully acknowledged: *Aeroplane Monthly* (for permission to use material from articles by the author originally published by them), *Aircraft Illustrated, Aviation Week*, British Aerospace, Warton, *The Doodlebugs* and *Hitler's Rockets*, both by Norman Longmate and published by Hutchinson, *From Blériot to Spitfire*, by David Ogilvy, published by Airlife, *Flight International*, and *Popular Flying* the Journal of the Popular Flying Association. Other sources used are Intelligence Summaries of HQ No 11 Group Fighter Command and No 122 Wing 2nd Tactical Air Force in the author's collection, RAF Fighter Command Combat Reports similarly in the author's collection, the author's own Pilot's Flying Log Book and *Luftwaffe Test Pilot*, by Hans Lerche, published by Jane's.

Acknowledgements

The author expresses grateful thanks to all who gave their generous assistance in the preparation of this book; and in particular to the Photographic Department, and to Chrys Butcher of the Flight Operations Department, of British Aerospace, Warton; to Joan Moores for coping with the typing with her exemplary skill and enthusiasm, and to his wife Pat for her untiring support and resolute proof-reading.

Additional thanks for the use of photographs from their respective collections go to: Aeritalia (colour page 7), Air Ministry (pages 152 and 155), British Aerospace (pages 27, 28, 39, 40, 41, 42, 43, 44, 46, 47, 51, 60, 61, 62, 70, 71, 72, 73, 74, 76, 77, 78, 80, 81, 82, 84, 85, 86, 87, 91, 93, 95, 96, 97, 100, 101, 102, 106, 110, 112, 114, 116, 118, 119, 122, 123, 124, 132, 133, 136, 137, colour pages 1, 5, 6, 7, 8, and facing title page), Dassault/Breguet (page 131), Bill Eaves (page 53), Flight International (pages 66 and 67), N Franks Collection (pages 25 and 26), Imperial War Museum (pages 10, 11, 12, 13, 26, 37, 38, 45, 47, and 48), Martin Co (pages 68 and 69), Ministry of Aviation (colour page 4), MOD (page 92), Ministry of Supply (page 74), MBB (page 138), PHT Green Collection (page 106), RAF Museum/Charles Brown (pages 23, 52 and 75), D Walker (page 64), Richard Wilson (colour pages 2 and 3) and Derek Wood (pages 65 and 66). Other photographs, author's collection.

Except where otherwise stated, all in-flight photographs show aircraft being flown by the author.

Chapter 1
Mayday!

On 7 March 1942, the spume-streaked North Sea below looked uninviting in the prevailing fierce north-easterly gale, and the yellow and white foaming waters over the Goodwins merged into the rain and sleet ahead when viewed from 200ft under the lowering cloud base. It was an uninspiring scene rendered even less attractive by the radiator temperature gauge in the cockpit of 609 Squadron Typhoon *PR-R*, which was oscillating and rising ominously. Confidence in the situation was further damaged by the insistent R/T voice of the writer's Belgian No 2, Van Lierde, saying 'Crooner Leader, bale out, you are streaming smoke'! Neither baling out nor ditching offered a pleasant prospect on that late winter day.

After a year or more of working with the Typhoon in factory trials and in squadron operations under an atmosphere of spreading lack of enthusiasm resulting from unreliability and frequent engine and structural failures, here was a personal moment of truth — it was at last happening to me and this Sabre engine was going to stop suddenly as soon as the radiator coolant boiled away. The vital question was, how long would it last?

The section of 609 Squadron Typhoons had been approaching the French coast on a 'Rhubarb' low-level sortie from Manston in marginal weather when the radiator gauge had begun to rise above normal and now, on the way back with the Goodwin sands below revealed only by the dense foam of the breaking storm waves, it was a question of whether the engine would last long enough for a forced landing to be made on dry land.

A ditching in the violent sea below became a progressively less attractive proposition as the engine grew hotter, but then a subtle change in the view through the rain-curtain ahead developed into a line of breakers and beyond them the lighter band of chalk cliffs, just as the radiator temperature went off the gauge.

With the propeller constant-speed lever at 'Full Coarse' to stretch the engine life, and with speed now down to 120mph, the stick was eased back to clear the cliff tops; but there was no power left, and with hot smells and shuddering vibration the propeller ground to a rigid stop with one blade vertical in front of the windscreen.

Now skimming the ground in heavy sleet, the fields beyond the cliff tops were only dimly visible and then, when bracing for a belly landing in the first suitable clear space, a church tower and small village appeared dead ahead. At less than 90mph, with little margin for manoeuvre above the stall, a bank to the right and a skating turn with heavy rudder just cleared the buildings and revealed a field ahead up the slope of a hill. Using all remaining control and finally with the stick hard back, the sloping field came up with a rush and the Typhoon hit tail-first with a resounding 'clunk'. The writer next remembers looking through the windscreen at stationary green grass to the accompaniment of sizzling noises, and thinking that he should have switched off fuel and ignition before now. This proved to be difficult, as did getting rid of the harness straps and climbing out. At this point it became noticeable that there was blood all over the place and events became blurred until, some time later, a voice said, 'Don't he look a bloody mess!' and kindly hands lifted the writer away from the wreck — which fortunately had not burned.

A short period followed in the excellent care of the Deal hospital staff, with time to reflect on the events which had led to this temporary inconvenience.

Chapter 2

Hurricanes into battle

Being posted to France in October 1939, the writer could not claim to have an expert opinion on Hurricane operations at that time when coming straight out from the RAF No 11 Group Fighter Pool at St Athan with the impressive total of 130 flying hours of which fifteen were on Hurricanes. But later, after six months in France and the ten days' fighting from 10 May 1940, one could claim to be almost a veteran.

In the winter of 1939, 87 Squadron was based on Lille Vendeville* aerodrome which consisted of an almost circular field of mud, one large old hangar, a group of wooden huts and an extraordinary monument to Gallic ingenuity in the shape of a towering wrought-iron platform mounted about 20ft above an enormous iron tank

which together did duty as the station latrine. In hot weather this produced an aroma needing experience to be believed and in the winds, rain, ice and snow of which there was plenty in that winter, its successful use was an exercise in extreme fortitude and dexterity; and so frequently was Hurricane flying in France at that time.

The wooden-hutted billets were far from draught-proof and kept little of the fearsome winter weather outside, so it was often a relief to climb into the cockpits of the Hurricanes and shut the canopies to keep the wind off. Flying during the early part of 1940 was restricted due to the tendency for all the airfields in northern France to become water-logged acres of black

* Later called Seclin.

Hurricanes of No 87 Squadron at Lille in 1939. The author is fourth from right among the pilots, running to his LK-L.

No 87 Squadron's first victory — a He 111 near Merville, November 1939. Dennis David on the wing.

mud, and on one occasion in January 1940 the whole squadron had to fly out from Lille to Le Touquet by taking off from the perimeter road as the airfield was in a totally impossible state.

To a new pilot the Hurricane was an immensely powerful but not excessively demanding aeroplane. Its wide track undercarriage, stable and responsive flying characteristics and reliable engine and hydraulic system resulted in a general atmosphere of confidence in the squadron, so that the newcomer had no reason to become apprehensive.

Getting lost over the flat agricultural plain of northern France in the generally unpleasant prevailing weather, in the total absence of radio nav-aids, was perhaps the only recurrent difficulty. But most of the flying consisted of formation practice and occasional patrols against reported enemy reconnaissance activity, and so one flew in sublime confidence that one's

No 87 Squadron pilots and ground crews with a panel from the squadron's first victory in World War 2: the Heinkel He 111 shot down from Lille in November 1939. Pilots from left to right are Squadron Leader Dewar, Dunn, Mackworth, David, Cowley, author, Glyde, Mitchel, Joyce and Rayner.

Left *The ground crew of Bobby Voase Jeff's Hurricane with the Heinkel Trophy*

Right *Squadron 'battle formation', 1940.*

formation leader knew precisely where he was. Hindsight suggests that this was seldom the case, and one was very well lost on one occasion when operating from Senan near Metz over the Maginot line in March 1940; after over two hours of flying around rather aimlessly the Section eventually landed at an airfield which turned out to be Nancy.

This airfield was situated at the base of the hill on which Nancy stands with a towering steeple near the summit. After the aircraft had been refuelled, the author took off solo again to return the short distance to base. Then the engine faltered and cut for a moment during the critical climb-out up the side of the hill over the roofs of Nancy. For a brief moment a crash-landing ahead amongst the houses seemed inevitable, but while bracing for this unpleasant possibility the engine picked up again and the Hurricane climbed laboriously at virtually street level up the high street of Nancy into the clear.

At about this time, while operating from Le Touquet, I had my first encounter with the enemy. This occurred one day in February 1940 when 87 Squadron was based at Le Touquet after our main airfield at Lille had become inoperable due to continuous rain and slush. Le Touquet had proved a hospitable spot and a champagne party was developing on the morning in question more or less as a continuation of the previous night's activity when the Readiness Section was scrambled.

This consisted of Australian 'Johnny' Cock and the writer (now with about 170 hours total flying time) with fixed-pitch Hurricane Is. As we strapped in hurriedly, the weather was noted to be far from convenient with solid low cloud and drizzle, and it was to be hoped that the unreliable TR9 radios would be of use when wanted. In the event mine was not, but soon committed over the cloud sheet in the Somme estuary area the Section was told to turn north-east and climb fast; shortly afterwards it was a surprise to see the unmistakable shape of a Heinkel 111 about 2,000ft above and climbing hard.

The Heinkel began to fire tracer at long range and the range was just beginning to close when the sky turned purple, vision became confused and the writer had time only to suspect oxygen starvation and push the nose down with controls centralized before virtually losing consciousness. Coming to just above the cloud sheet and feeling decidedly out of contact with what was going on, I slid back the canopy for fresh air. A jerk followed with the eventual discovery that the oxygen hose was missing, having been disconnected at the bayonet joint where I had apparently failed to check it in the hurry to take off. Then when calling for a homing over the unbroken cloud sheet, the aforesaid TR9

produced no recognizable assistance and left me to sort out the situation.

Deciding that a let-down over the sea was the only safe course, this was carried out on a south-westerly heading, finally breaking cloud at very low level over a smooth grey sea and heading back north along the sand dunes of the French coast to Le Touquet where John Cock was already back, having thought that he had shot the Heinkel down or at least seen it disappear diving steeply into the cloud cover.

When all-out war started on 10 May 1940 the Hurricanes of the Air Component were soon heavily engaged and began to be reinforced from the UK; but they continued to sail into battle in the immaculate squadron formation of those days and sometimes got clobbered badly in the process.

In my second combat, 87 Squadron in three Vics of three intercepted a formation of Dornier 17s with Me 110 escorts near Maastricht, and the battle immediately broke up into a mêlée of individual combats. 'B' Flight had been sitting (by the Hurricanes) in the ditch which served as the Flight Dispersal at Lille Marcq, and sounds of gunfire and bombs had indicated activity in the direction of Lille. Then, very high and barely in sight in the afternoon glare, a small white parachute was seen. This turned out to be a pilot of 85 Squadron from Seclin, but before the end of

his descent the Ops telephone suddenly shrilled and 87 was off to patrol Maastricht at 18,000ft.

The field was too small for the whole squadron to be parked on one side and theoretically one Flight took off after the other, but in this event twelve Hurricanes thundered at each other from opposite ends as they gathered speed ponderously behind their huge fixed-pitch propellers — a hump in the middle of the field ensuring that no-one could judge if someone from the other Flight was on a collision course until both were converging on the hump at a combined speed of about 150mph. But there were no collisions and after a fleeting impression of other aircraft flashing by on either side, all the Hurricanes were clear and closing into formation in a long climbing turn towards the east.

As the squadron closed up an indistinct radio message indicated activity in the Brussels area and after about ten minutes, directly ahead and a little above, a formation of big aircraft was seen crossing from left to right. 87 continued at full power until the aircraft ahead became recognizable as Dornier 17 bombers. There was no moment for hesitation; with the gunsight ON and gun button to FIRE the author then ruddered the gunsight on to the nearest bomber in a 30° deflection astern attack and opened fire with a long burst. I was still alongside flight commander Voase Jeff's Hurricane, and he said later that 'You opened fire miles out of range as I wasn't in range myself and you were behind me!'

All that mattered at that point, though, was to get in at the enemy, and then the immediate sky became full of small twin-engine aeroplanes with twin fins, Me 110s. There was no time for tactics or formation drill and while breaking into a hard port turn instinctively, a '110 went by close behind. A further maximum power tight turn to port brought the writer out of the immediate mêlée and then ahead was a Hurricane diving away with a '110 close behind him streaming gunfire smoke. It was well out of range and when I started to give chase, ahead and crossing from right to left appeared a Dornier on its own, nose down for home with twin trails of smoke from its full-throttle engines.

Flying due east, down to 10,000ft and not gaining much ground, a long range burst with one ring vertical deflection from the eight Brownings caused the Dornier's port engine to stop with smoke and a sharp yaw. Now closing quickly, a short burst from close range dead astern put the Dornier into a vertical dive into the low cloud at 2,000ft.

Being almost certainly well into enemy territory by now, alone and above a revealing white cloud sheet, I began to feel somewhat insecure and so, after diving through the cloud, I set a north-westerly heading over the rolling forests of the Ardennes. Presently the trees gave way to ploughed land and while looking for landmarks we were suddenly bracketed by shell bursts, some of which were too close for comfort. It was impossible to tell whether they were 'friendly' or otherwise and immaterial in the circumstances. This also seemed unhealthy though, so a further dive to low level over the fields to provide a less sitting target was called for. This produced no more flak, but now lines of tracer fire from behind! A hasty sideslip and a quick look over the left shoulder and there not 200yd away was another Dornier with his front gunner having some quite effective target practice.

A full throttle tight left turn at treetop height soon reversed the position and, although this German flew his bomber with surprising skill and tenacity, in less than two turns the Hurricane was coming round on to his tail and then, with the engine boost override pulled, banking into position for a broad deflection shot.

With the Dornier in a perfect position for this at under 200yd range and his top rear gunner now also opening fire, I pressed the gun button. Three rounds went off, then silence. Now there was a predicament. This worthy bomber pilot whose aeroplane was almost as fast as the Hurricane in this ground level combat, had been outmanoeuvred. He had three gun positions with an unknown amount of ammunition remaining, while the Hurricane had eight guns and no ammunition, and the moment the Hurricane broke the circle from behind the Dornier's tail the German could 'jump' the Hurricane again unless something could be thought out quickly.

Closing in under his tail and trying to keep between the fields of fire of his upper and lower guns, all the Hurricane's manoeuvrability and full over-boost power was used to roll away to the right from the left-hand circle, and then the nose was pushed down to 50ft above the fields on a northerly heading. On looking round, this determined German could be seen banking round vertically to level out some way behind and fire a few more bursts from his front gun at steadily increasing range. Then, as the Hurricane drew away, the Dornier pulled up, rocking his wings before turning away to the east. He had scored a moral victory undoubtedly, but the writer was at least still around to have another go at his friends!

The next combat was a classic example of the weakness of inflexibility.

No 87 Squadron was now operating full-time from the grass field at Lille Marcq and had been ordered off with two reinforcing squadrons from the UK to patrol the ground battle area at Valencienne at 10,000ft. It was a fine sight as 36 Hurricanes formed up in the late afternoon sun in three squadron 'boxes' line-astern, four sections of Vic threes to a squadron.

The writer was flying No 2 in the right-hand section of 87 squadron, leading the wing, and it made one feel quite brave looking back at so many friendly fighters; and then without fuss or drama about ten Me 109s appeared above the left rear flank of our formation out of some high cloud.

The Wing leader, 'Johnny' Dewar, turned in towards them as fast as a big formation could be wheeled, but the '109s abandoned close drill and, pulling their turn tight, dived one after the other on to the tail sections of the Wing. Their guns streamed smoke and one by one four Hurricanes

The author 'running up' his Hurricane during the Battle of Britain.

fell away. None of us fired a shot, some never even saw it happen, and the enemy disengaged while we continued to give a massive impression of combat strength over the battle area with four less Hurricanes than when we started.

We had had more than three times the strength of the enemy on this occasion, and had been soundly beaten tactically by a much smaller unit led with flexibility and resolution.

The Battle of France was soon over but the authorities were slow to react to facts and change the rules, and change came about the hard way by squadrons learning from experience and adapting themselves. Nevertheless, there were still some squadrons going into action in the beginning of the Battle of Britain in 'standard Fighter Command attacks', and many in the inflexible three sections Vic formation.

No 87 Squadron had modified tactics to an initial turn in towards the enemy when sighted followed by flexible exploitation of the subsequent situation; in other words, every man for himself. The Squadron still flew in three Vics of three, but in extended battle formation with wingmen 'weaving' for cross reference; at no time was close No 2 cover practised though, nor the basic 'finger-four' formation flown by the Germans and adopted by the RAF too late at the end of the battle.

One of the most effective tactics used by our side was the head-on 'into the brown' manoeuvre. The author had experience of this on 15 August over Portland when, still with 87 and now flying

out of Exeter, Squadron Leader Lovell Grieg led the Squadron straight into the starboard front of a dense mass of Ju 87s with Me 110 escorts which the RDF★ had reported as '120' plus'. This seemed quite eminently believable and the resultant somewhat unco-ordinated plunge right through the middle of this armada seemed to put them off their bomb-aiming more than somewhat, in addition to destroying a number of them. Lovell Grieg did not return from this action.

Another of these great battles took place over Warmwell and Weymouth on 25 August when 87 took on '100 plus' Ju 88s, Do 17s and Me 109 escorts, and after 'browning' a couple of Dorniers the writer succeeded in forcing a '109 to belly-land on fire close behind Chesil Beach at Abbotsbury †.

And so into September and early October when the numbers and intensity of the daylight attacks were clearly becoming less. Up east, the Biggin Hill, Tangmere, Northolt, Kenley and North Weald wings were still having a hard time, but replacements were beating the losses and the tide was turning! In all this, and despite the torrent of rhetoric and euphoria that has poured out in the intervening years apportioning credit here and blame there for the conduct of the battle, the central theme in Fighter Command was the extraordinary morale.

★ Radio Direction Finding, later called Radar.
† See Appendix 2.

Viewed from forty years on and in times of much changed values, the calm casualness of the squadron and flight commanders as they daily controlled their units in the bombed and strafed dispersals of the fighter stations, seemed totally unaffected by the realities of the daily losses and ever-increasing personal dangers. Many had long since dismissed any idea that they might survive this fight, and were totally dedicated to taking as many of the enemy with them as they could.

The 'form' at every station and in every squadron was not that we were in any sort of difficult situation, but that this was what the RAF was for — to defend the country (which was unquestionably worth defending) against this brutal enemy — and as fighter pilots we were the most privileged people in the land at this time. The RAF was going to win, and 'our squadron' was showing everyone the way!

There was a total absence of dramatics or false heroics — indeed, to be other than casual and apparently unimpressed by all that was going on was to be out of line and rather uncomfortable.

On duty the daily 'scrambles' were faced with apparent eagerness and humour by all — no matter if some felt desperate, they were even more determined not to show it — and then after the battle and the 'Release from Readiness' at the end of the day came the time for easing of tensions — the laughter, the parties, the sheer good-humoured enjoyment of the company of friends who had shared the same dangers and would again tomorrow.

All right, you might 'buy it' in the end, but your job was tremendous in the best squadron in the best air force; flying fighters was wonderful and we were beating the Krauts! What more could anyone ask?

This morale stemmed directly from the matter-of-fact approach to Service responsibility fostered with such success by the RAF between the wars, and it was quietly, deliberately but never ostentatiously, promoted by the 25-year-old Squadron Leaders and twenty-year-old Flight Lieutenants as the battle reached its grimmest, when losses became so high that some squadrons

Right *An 87 Squadron Hurricane I with 'Watty' Watson at Exeter in August 1940.*

Left *A great fighter leader. Squadron Leader 'Johnny' Dewar at 'Readiness' with 87 Squadron, Exeter 1940.*

only lasted for a week or so before being pulled out to re-man and re-train.

Morale was, of course, the key to success and in these present times of differing standards it may be hard for some to understand that for many of the survivors of the 1940 air battles, their lasting memories of the time were not so much the fears but the fun. The laughter on and off-duty, the sense of pride in our Service, and the joy of flying. These were for many the best times of their lives.

In the spring and summer of 1940, although without the elegance and high altitude performance of the Spitfire, the Hurricane was a machine of its time and many of us would not have changed it for any other mount. We knew it as a rugged, stable, forgiving aeroplane which was tolerant of our clumsiness and the worst that the weather could do. It absorbed legendary amounts of enemy fire and kept flying — we could hit the target well with its eight guns, and when in trouble we felt that we could outfly the enemy's best.

The Hurricane and the Spitfire made a great team, but I never regretted my posting to a Hurricane squadron in that fateful time and later was proud to take part in testing many new production machines at the great Hawker factory at Langley.

Chapter 3

Hurricanes at night

The onset of winter 1940/41 was a strange period for 87 Squadron which had spent the previous six months in the thick of the day fighting in Northern France and Belgium; then, after a short pause for breath, beer and re-equipment in the tranquillity of the Yorkshire countryside at Church Fenton, went back into what was almost immediately to develop into the right flank of the Battle of Britain, from Exeter.

Pilot losses in France in May and then through July, August and September in major battles over the Channel from Portland to Portsmouth had totalled more than fifty per cent, including two fine commanding officers, 'Johnny' Dewar and Terry Lovell Grieg; but we gave as good as we got or better and by October, with the emerging realization that the Luftwaffe had been defeated, morale which had been inspiring and unfaltering throughout the summer's battles was sky-high indeed.

At that point movement orders were received to base the Squadron at a new satellite airfield of RAF Colerne near Bath called Charmy Down, after some intermediate operations from the grass airfield at Bibury from where we had carried out periodic moonlight patrols over Bristol during the past few weeks.

This looked ominous, and it was soon confirmed that 87 was indeed to become a full-time night-fighter squadron! This prospect

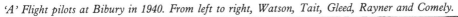

'A' Flight pilots at Bibury in 1940. From left to right, Watson, Tait, Gleed, Rayner and Comely.

Cowley, 'Rubber' Thoroughgood and Rayner at Bibury.

seemed disastrous to a bunch of day-fighter pilots who had not only survived the two great air defence actions of the war so far but had done so with, they considered, a very positive share in the ultimate victory. As they now saw it they had to give up the inspiring climbs in formation into the brilliant skies above cloud to fight and throw back an arrogant enemy whose black-swastikad hordes had daily trespassed over our land and homes, and instead live a life of crouching in the dark in ill-heated huts awaiting the Op's telephone call to 'Patrol Line A at 10,000ft'; an order which would lead to a lone flight into the darkness in whatever the weather happened to be when the order was issued — 10 Group Headquarters' comforting observation in this connection being already well known: 'If the Hun is flying so can you!'

It was an enormous contrast and it said much

'B' Flight commander Derek Ward with Mrs Rigby, the pilots' billet owner at North Leach, and Jay in the squadron Tiger Moth at Bibury in September 1940. Trevor Jay had just flown Mrs Rigby.

for RAF training, as night bombing was seen to be the new threat to this country following the failure of the German air forces against Fighter Command in daytime, that 87 and the other squadrons concerned just got down to the new job as best they could. But this was not too well. There were no effective homing aids at the beginning and each sortie had to be conducted by DR (watch and compass) navigation to and from the patrol line which, in theory, could be seen from 10,000ft as groups of flares at ten-mile intervals.

In practice of course, the flares could only be seen on very clear nights which seldom happen over this country in the winter. So the patrols were flown by timed runs on reciprocal headings and in the cases of all but the most skilled in pilot navigation, after $1\frac{1}{2}$ hours on patrol on a pitch dark night and over cloud or mist there were few pilots who had much of an idea of their position.

Then, in theory, a 'fix' should have been possible by 'triangulation' on radio voice transmissions. In practice the TR9 radios were so unreliable and sensitive to atmospheric conditions that the night fighter pilot would have to resort to setting the 'safety course' for his home beacon at the end of his $1\frac{1}{2}$-hour patrol and then begin his descent, hoping to break out below cloud at the end of a timed run in sight of the beacon flashing his base signal — or any other beacon which would lead him to somewhere to land before his fuel ran out!

Once on patrol, of course, it was a case of eyeballing with no radar through a thick armourglass windscreen surrounded by heavy metal structure (and past the reflector gunsight with bright aiming spot and graticules when switched on), and the sighting of and holding on to another aircraft in the darkness was supremely difficult. The majority of our few interceptions in that winter were in fact on searchlight-illuminated targets or following fleeting glimpses of bombers silhouetted against the massive fires of the cities of Bristol, Swansea, Plymouth or London burning below.

Nevertheless, the job was tackled with intense effort and what would nowadays be called 'professionalism'. Specific training was carried out on every suitable night by pilots not on standby, and included local and cross-country formation flying in moonlight and full darkness and, of particular importance, pairs flying to assess each other's limits of night visibility by the No 2 dropping slowly astern of the leader until firstly the latter's silhouette disappeared at about 400yd, and then the blue exhaust flames became almost invisible. Inevitably sometimes contact was lost, and in all these sorties DR navigation over a totally blacked-out countryside was the sole means of recovery to a safe landing.

The enthralling vistas of the day fighter pilot in wide open skies had been replaced for us by the confines of the dimly red-lit cockpit with often nothing distinguishable in the total darkness outside. Then our whole existence seemed limited to this and the thunderous vibrations of the Merlin engine on whose continued roar life indeed depended, for as our recent experience indicated parachute escape from the Hurricane was by no means an assured way out.

Clear moonlight or even very clear starlight nights were a pleasure as navigation could generally be visual on the outlines of the Severn, or on occasions Plymouth Sound or the Thames; but in all other circumstances of darkness in mist, rain, thick cloud, icing and snow, all of which occurred in plenty in that winter at Charmy Down, the uncertainty was dominant until, sometimes after casting around in a black goldfish bowl at the lowest altimeter height considered safe relative to the hills one might be over, the mist to one side or ahead began to glow intermittently with the signal of a flashing beacon. Then, turn up the cockpit rheostat, check the beacon signal against the beacon card for the bearing to the airfield, set the new course and begin final descent; when below 500ft, the line of shrouded paraffin flares would appear one after the other ahead. Undercarriage and flaps down, sometimes a hurried S turn to line up and then throttle closed, stick back, sparks each side from the throttled engine, and then the thump of a hard arrival or less frequently a gentle three-pointer and no more to do but try to keep straight between the flares, which was not all that easy in a crosswind in the wet.

A brief handover to the loyal ground crew who would service one aircraft after another all through the night in the open whatever the fierce weather; and so back to the generally bitter-cold dispersal hut for a hot cup of tea and a lie down under a blanket for the rest of the night or until one's turn for another patrol, this time with luck to return more easily in the light of the dawn.

It was a challenge every night, but although the risk of accident was high and many aircraft and some pilots were lost that winter, the chances of operational success were low and very few interceptions occurred, most of which were inconclusive. The writer fired at two Ju 88s over Bristol in the searchlights during a five month period, and both plots disappeared over the Severn and were recorded as 'probably destroyed'. But when 'Splinters' Smallwood saw some navigation lights over the middle of a major raid on Bristol one night and dived to investigate, he found 'a clot of a Heinkel' and shot it down over land.

It was slow going, and by the spring of 1941 with the news that the Spitfire wings were taking the offensive and beginning 'the sweeping season' over France, 87 sought other outlets from the dreary round of night 'Politician Patrols'. The energetic CO, 'Widge' Gleed, obtained tentative and rather surprised support from No 10 Group Headquarters at Rudloe Manor for two experimental operations, the future of either of which was to depend 'strictly on results'; which meant that in the event of initial failure there would be no second chances.

One plan was to send a detachment to a small grass airfield on St Mary's in the Scilly Isles for the purpose of daylight interception of enemy mine-laying and reconnaissance sorties which had been reported in the area in some numbers by Intelligence. The second plan was, for that time, an unusual and some thought extremely radical one of employing our new-found confidence in night operations in ground-attacks by moonlight on enemy airfields.

By the spring of 1941 following its long, hard winter of night operations and a training syllabus which had even included regular night formation aerobatics, 87 Squadron felt ready to extend its new-found expertise and on 9 April the first of these new operations was mounted.

Squadron Leader Ian Gleed led four aircraft to Warmwell at dusk for refuelling, and then a long wait until the take-off time planned for the first sortie. The plan involved the CO, and his usual No 2, 'Rubber' Thoroughgood, reconnoitring the area of Caen-Carpiquet airfield south-east of the Cherbourg peninsula and attacking 'targets of opportunity' if the nearly-full moon gave sufficient visibility. If the defences were active and included searchlights, each aircraft would

attempt to cover the other by strafing.

No-one knew if ground-attack with 0.303-in machine-guns would be practical by moonlight. The object was to find out, and if the CO's sortie was successful Derek Ward and the writer would make a follow-up attack. This was to be not only the squadron's first night ground attack, but probably the first by any single-engine fighters in World War 2.

At Warmwell in the stillness of the otherwise deserted aerodrome, the moon rose in a cloudless sky over the Purbeck Hills and the chill of a heavy dew heralded a frost later, leading to practical thoughts of keeping windscreen and wings protected. Then start-up time approached and the first two Merlins crackled into life, shattering the stillness. Presently they taxied out over the rough grass, turned into wind and thundered off in loose formation, extinguishing navigation lights as they turned south under the now bright moon.

Ward and the writer prepared for a long two-hour wait for the first pair to return and for confirmation that the next sortie would be on; but as we were entering the cold Mess building, otherwise deserted on this day-fighter station, the unmistakable sound of a Merlin approaching brought us back to the 'Flights' in a hurry and in time to see *LK-A*, Gleed's Hurricane, swing round and switch-off.

He slid back the hood as we climbed up on the wing and said, 'Got a bloody great Dornier off Lulworth! Where's "Rubber"?' But then the other Hurricane curved in down the moon path, and in an hilarious de-briefing it transpired that hardly had they settled down on course for Normandy at about 10,000ft than Gleed had glimpsed a dark shape going past in the opposite direction and, turning sharply, had seen exhaust flames against the stars, closed and opened fire on a clearly recognized Dornier 17.

Thoroughgood, meanwhile, had lost his leader in this manoeuvre but then saw a fire going down and hitting the sea, so he also came back.

Gleed, having had one successful sortie and now experiencing delay in re-arming, was of a mind to try the offensive operation on another night, but New Zealander Derek Ward with our two Hurricanes fully armed and ready was not to be put off, and it was decided that the second sortie would go ahead as planned — so the second section would now do the exploratory work!

With a brilliant moon and a stable weather forecast all was favourable, and after a loose formation take-off over the undulating Warmwell grass and setting course on the climb for France, station keeping in the moonlight was as easy as in daylight. With eighty miles of water ahead the customary illusion of engine roughness soon occurred, to be disciplined after a close scrutiny of the perfectly healthy engine instruments.

Night cross-country formation flying carried no mystery for us and the writer, flying No 2, relaxed in the comfortable knowledge that the leader's navigation would be accurate. Sufficient to cross-check only at the first visual check point on crossing the enemy coast to ensure a good 'safety course' for the likely solo return, because visual contact with the leader would most likely be lost over the target.

The two Hurricanes droned steadily on at 10,000ft and then, indistinctly at first and soon with final definition, a thin dark line to starboard revealed the Cherbourg coast curving round eastwards towards the Normandy beaches ahead. The enemy coast, and time to tighten the harness straps, check engine and fuel gauges, switch on gunsight with rheostat set low hopefully for ground-attack, and then finally turn the gun button on the spade-grip from 'Safe' to 'Fire'.

With the coastline clear below, Ward's Hurricane began to lose height gently, holding course for Carpiquet which should come up in four minutes. Down to 2,000ft, then with final confirmation of target area two brilliant blue searchlights snapped on and weaved almost horizontally ahead in agitated scan.

Breaking radio silence Ward called 'there's the aerodrome' and dived down to port. Ahead the flak defences erupted in chains of tracer weaving haphazardly at first, but then one of the searchlights illuminated the leading Hurricane followed by another and it looked for all the world like a moth twisting in a car's headlights.

Here was the No 2's task, and rolling down on to the source of the nearest searchlight I aimed directly at it and fired a long burst with first the tracer rounds and then the 'de Wilde' flashing explosive rounds, confirming accuracy. With breath-taking suddenness the light snapped out leaving a dying glow which helped judgement of pull-up, and then 'snap' — the other light swung right on from almost dead ahead. In the dazzling bluish glare nothing could be read in the cockpit,

and though at very low altitude the ground was invisible. Tracer shells now began to whip by with a pronounced 'whoomph whoomph', and the only possible action was to aim and fire straight down the beam, knowing that this was the classically dangerous maneouvre as it would destroy 'night vision' for probably a fatal period if and when the light went out.

After a seemingly endless burst, but in reality a very few seconds, the dazzle snapped out to blackness, again with the dying glow of the light helping the writer to avoid flying right into it; then a snatched pull on the stick with a fleeting impression of objects flashing by on each side before regaining some sort of re-orientation in a shallow climb with the moon in the right place and the altimeter now perceived to read 300ft and climbing.

But where was the target? Over to port converging chains of tracer shells showed where Ward might be, and immediately lines of machine-gun tracer pouring downwards showed his attack on something — then a flash of fire on the ground. There were no searchlights now and, quickly aiming for the fire and diving down through 200ft, I saw the moonlight suddenly glint on runways, hangars and the shapes of parked aircraft by the now raging fire.

With gunsight aiming-spot near the fire, a continuous gun-burst strafing run was made through what looked like parked Me 109s, and on into a hangar before clearing low over the latter as the Brownings stuttered out of ammunition to silence. Then low down and pursued briefly by chains of tracer shells and bullets over shadowy fields, woods, a railway line with red-lit signals, then a glinting canal and with final relief the light strip of beach at the coast before pulling up at climb power to set course for the planned recovery base, Middle Wallop, with only a single searchlight still weaving behind.

On the climb a disturbing hot smell caused swift study of the engine panel and outside for any signs of battle damage, although no hits had been felt; but all was well and the smell was recognized as cordite smoke from the Brownings.

Crossing out had been on planned time and now the navigation had to be good to find the new landing base, Middle Wallop. A brief radio call to Ward produced only silence and worry — his aircraft should not be far away, so had he been hit?

The CO's aircraft of No 87 Squadron in 'night black' flying from Charmy Down in 1941.

Under the still clear moon, but in haze up to 8,000ft, the sky and sea below seemed to merge and only in a look back did the moon path on the sea confirm that there was no cloud below. Holding course at 10,000ft for half an hour seemed ages longer and then in a gentle descent the greyness ahead was searched for a sign of land. A recognizable pin-point was important for confirmation of heading to the Wallop beacon.

Suddenly a faint white line appeared to starboard — this seemed wrong as it should have been the chalk cliffs of Purbeck at Swanage's Old Harry Rocks to port. This had to be the Isle of Wight at the Needles, and descent rate was increased to ensure a better view of the mainland crossing-in, but in the haze this couldn't be seen.

Nothing to do but hold course until within radio range of Wallop and then suddenly — duck! A large black shape loomed ahead and rushed down the starboard side. Then another straight ahead and a third above to port. In the concentration on events the Southampton balloon barrage had been completely forgotten! In clear weather they flew to above 5,000ft and a glance at the altimeter showed 4,500ft!

With full throttle and 'fine' pitch the Hurricane was stood on its tail and with fleeting glimpses of more balloons, this time their silvered tops seen from level and above glinting in the moon, the danger was past.

Ahead a flashing beacon reading the code for Wallop, and soon the Hurricane was bumping down the strange grass flare-path. The time was 02:00 and at dispersal (John Cunningham's Beaufighters) no news was to be had of Ward. While *LK-L* was being refuelled and re-armed, experiences were exchanged with the AI-equipped Beaufighter pilots who were intrigued to hear about our attempts at 'eyeballing' enemy aircraft at night and the night ground attacks in the single-engined Hurricane — they thought we were mad on both counts.

Then a short, relaxed, fifteen-minute flight back to Bath under the still bright moon, to land on the Charmy Down flarepath before dawn and to find Derek Ward already there after returning via Warmwell where he had landed to check for possible flak damage.

He said 'Thanks for shooting that searchlight off me "Boo" it was great we must try that again!' As indeed we did on 7 May, again from Warmwell when the writer led an attack on the Me 109 airfield at Maupertus on Cherbourg in *LK-L* (serial *V7285*) with Peter Roscoe flying No 2.

On this sortie there was no difficulty in seeing runways and buildings in the moonlight, but we could not identify aircraft easily or other detailed targets at first and the searchlights and flak were very active and accurate; so both aircraft fired at gunposts and searchlights briefly before attacking the parked aircraft finally seen near the hangars, and then disengaged discreetly.

Shortly after crossing out over the coast a brief

winking signal light revealed the white 'V' of a fast vessel travelling west close in to the shore. On the assumption that it might be an E-boat, *LK-L* was eased into a diving turn to line up the target against the moon path. This worked out, and at a few hundred feet and an estimated 1,000yd the low profile of a fast patrol boat could be easily seen in silhouette, and fire was opened and continued to point blank range with de Wilde hits sparking all round the bridge area and tracer ricocheting upwards ahead.

The ammunition ran out as the Hurricane cleared close overhead and was held low in a tight left bank away from the moon as late return tracer fire erupted from one or two gun positions. But soon these fell away behind and course was set for Warmwell which was reached uneventfully.

The most hazardous part of the operation however, occurred back at Warmwell an hour later after refuelling and re-arming when during take-off over white-frosted grass towards the misty Purbeck Hills the right wing dropped violently, heavy vibration set in accompanied by a rumbling roar and nearly full left stick was suddenly required even to hold the wings level. Despite the indistinct light of the moon the cause of the trouble was evident — a large dark hole in the top surface of the starboard wing showed where the whole gun servicing panel on that side had disappeared. So the problem was two-fold — how to make a safe landing, and where!

Some experimenting showed that with undercarriage down and no flap, aileron control of the wing-drop ran out below 100mph, and this would mean a fast landing although flap could be lowered once the wheels were on the ground. It was therefore decided that the longer runway of Charmy Down would be better for this sort of arrival, and it would also be less complicated to do it at home! So course was set for Bath in gathering moon haze which was not helpful, but after some anxious moments the home beacon was eventually found, periodically illuminating the murk ahead. Then a long, flat approach was made on the bearing for Charmy Down whose flarepath thankfully appeared out of the haze at about a mile ahead.

At 110mph the left stick load was becoming nearly unbearable, and when the threshold lights flashed by underneath the flaps were selected just as the main wheels touched in a tail-high 'wheeler'. With the red 'glim lamps' of the

runway end approaching rapidly, maximum possible braking was applied short of nosing over and then with hard left rudder the Hurricane was slithered sideways to stop off the runway on the frosty grass overshoot area.

There was no further damage and, after a look at the wing, the Flight Sergeant subsequently passed some crisp advice to the Warmwell station armourers about how to fasten gun panels; but this sortie had given further confidence to the theory that fighters could be used in offensive operations at night and that ground targets could be identified and attacked in good moonlight.

The short range of 0.303-in machine-guns and low lethality meant that these operations were of questionable value apart from waking up the enemy, but we had at least shown that with heavier armament it could be a different story.

Meanwhile a new diversion occurred for 87 Squadron whose indefatigable CO caused a 450yd strip to be marked out on Charmy Down. He then told each flight commander to select four pilots and train them to operate their Hurricanes safely and in bad weather within these take-off and landing limits. With practice this was just within the Hurricane's capabilities, and so on 20 May 1941 six aircraft flown by Gleed, Ward, Badger, Thoroughgood, Rayner and the writer set off under low cloud and rain for St Mary's on the Scilly Isles.

I had never seen the Scillies before and, circling in the rain over Hugh Town, watched Gleed's leading aircraft with interest as it slanted down towards what looked like an impossibly small field on the edge of the cliffs above the town.

The Hurricane dragged low over the rocks, touched short on the grass and slithered down to a stop impressively close to a line of short, wind-bent trees which marked the aerodrome boundary. Then it was my turn, and with power set to 'trickle' in at 85mph the wheels were lifted over the rocky cliff edge and planted firmly with chopped throttle on to the grass. Only then did the steepness of the downslope towards the trees become apparent, but the last of the heavily braked energy was killed by kicking on left rudder and skidding the Hurricane to a stop with the wing tip almost in the trees.

Then came the other two aircraft, also with no room to spare, and after instructing the ground party that 'Readiness' next day would be from 'first light', Gleed prepared to go down to the

Lunch at 'Readiness' on the Scilly Isles, May 1941. From left to right, Rayner, author, Watson and John Strachey (the Squadron adjutant and post-war Labour Minister).

town to find our billets. At this point a red flare appeared from the direction of the Coastguard Station followed by another; this was the agreed coded signal to indicate 'enemy aircraft in sight north-east'.

Of the four Hurricanes, three were being refuelled and serviced with panels off, and only Badger's was still available. He leapt into his cockpit, started up and in a cloud of exhaust smoke, twigs and bits of grass, charged back up the slope downwind and disappeared from sight over the cliffs. For an awful moment it seemed that he might have gone in, but then came a clear, sustained burst of multiple machine-gun fire, a pause and then another burst.

In astonished silence we waited for a few minutes and then with a sudden rumble of sound the Hurricane appeared low over the headland, swept round the airfield and landed bumpily down the slope. This time pilots and ground crew were organized in groups to meet it and catch hold of the wing tips to help prevent over-running. Blackened gunports showed evidence of combat.

Sliding back his canopy as the Merlin spluttered to silence, and grinning broadly, Peter Badger reported to the CO 'There were two

Dornier 22 float planes just below the headland — I nearly fell on to one of them as I cleared the cliffs!' He had shot one into the sea, and the other had got away in the low cloud.

This was a good start to 'Operation Fishing', as the St Mary's detachment was code-named, and there was some celebrating that night in Hugh Town. But this did not prevent Gleed and Thoroughgood coming to 'Readiness' on the aerodrome at dawn the next day, still in low cloud and rain; and the rest of the pilots were astonished when at breakfast in their boarding-house billet in the town, to hear a sudden roar of engines and then many bursts of machine-gun fire.

The 'Readiness Section' had scrambled to investigate coastguard flares again and had chased a three-engined Dornier 18 flying-boat right across St Mary's at a few hundred feet, shooting it down just off the coast.

So began a welcome diversion for the 87 'night fighters' who continued the detached flight at St Mary's with frequent successes against enemy reconnaissance, shipping raiders and mine-layers for the next six months. Subsequently the confidence gained in the 1940/41 winter of night and bad weather operations opened the field for wider and more varied operations for fighters in

the future, and when in 1942 the then-new Hawker Typhoon was getting itself a bad name as a high altitude day fighter and was under consideration for cancellation, the writer, by then CO of No 609 (WR) Squadron, was authorized to try it out in as many varied rôles as was thought practical. Drawing on 87 Squadron experiences, these trials soon included night interception and formation, daylight ground-attack in bad weather, moonlight ground-attack on rail targets and shipping attacks by day and night. In all these the Typhoon's heavy 20mm cannon armament provided the punch to cause real damage up to a useful 1,000yd range, in contrast to the 0.303-in machine-guns of the Hurricane I.

In a two-month period from December 1942 the Typhoons of 609 made over 100 successful attacks on trains by moonlight, in addition to maintaining a mounting pressure of successful daylight low-level attacks on rail, canal, transport and airfield targets. The Typhoon was reprieved in 1943 with its rôle changed from day-interceptor fighter to that of the standard low-level ground attack fighter of the RAF for the coming invasion of Europe in which it provided a most successful and often vital contribution.

Chapter 4

Typhoon trials

I had first seen the prototype Typhoons with Napier Sabre engines and Tornados with Rolls-Royce Vultures at Hawker's Langley factory in December 1941, and their absurdly inadequate cockpit transparencies had made an unfavourable impression on this operational fighter pilot. Forward vision might be just marginally acceptable, but the pilot was virtually blind to the rear. Apparently the specification for this new interceptor fighter had called for a speed approaching 100mph faster than existing fighters, and a comment that 'the pilot would not need to look back!'

Similar situations have recurred in British fighter designs ever since the end of the open-cockpit era, and apart from pressure from operational units towards the end of World War 2 which produced excellent canopies (after the Fw 190 had shown the way) for production series

Typhoons, Tempests and Spitfires, the trend has been generally to provide less than optimum vision in our fighters. It has been left to the jet combat-experienced Americans to re-learn this lesson and virtually surround the 1980s' fighter pilots in 'glass' in their advanced F-15, F-16 and F-18 fighters. But in 1942 this was a major problem. The Typhoon test programme at Hawkers at Langley was progressing under difficult technical circumstances, with Chief Test Pilot Philip Lucas in charge and Ken Seth Smith as No 2 experimental pilot. Engine unreliability had caused much trouble, and other problems had included a near-catastrophic structural failure of the rear fuselage of the first prototype, *P5212*, which Lucas had miraculously landed safely and for which he was subsequently awarded a George Medal.

The prototype Typhoons seen at Langley amid

Hawker Tornado prototype P5224 *with Rolls-Royce Vulture engine.*

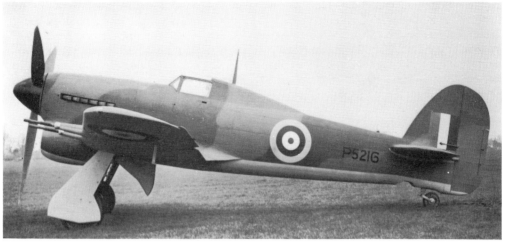

The second prototype Hawker Typhoon Ib (cannon-armed) at Langley in 1941.

the mass production of Hurricane IIs were aggressive, ungainly and very noisy aeroplanes, but their speed potential and heavy armament of twelve 0.303-in machine-guns for the Mk Ia or four 20mm cannon on the Mk Ib would surely be of value in at least some limited types of operation. However it was already becoming apparent that with their disappointing altitude performance the Typhoons would be no match for the developed Spitfires, Fw 190s and late-model Me 109s above 20,000ft.

The writer was engaged in Hurricane production testing in 1942 on a 'rest period' attachment from Fighter Command, and after flying the Tornado prototypes *P5219, HG641* and *R7939* in February, an opportunity to start Typhoon testing came with a flight on 8 March in *R7681,* a series Ia with twelve machine-guns.

This proved to be a surprise for once it was established that the noise, vibration and general commotion caused by the big Sabre engine and enhanced by the draughty cockpit with rattling 'wind-up' side windows were not actually breaking or stopping anything, it was soon apparent that the aeroplane was pleasantly stable and responsive to controls in all axes, very manoeuvrable (and exceptionally so for that period at speeds above 400mph), and it had a tremendous turn of speed. A 75 per cent power low-level cruise at over 300mph was fast for those days as was a maximum power 'level' of 385mph; and at the advertised dive limit of 500mph there was adequate control remaining, though with heavy control forces and a most impressive noise level.

It began to look as if this heavy and noisy

The original Typhoons were virtually 'blind' to the rear.

aeroplane could meet a number of operating rôles other than those specified for it, while being pleasant to fly in the process.

A look at low speed handling and the stall confirmed the briefing that controllability was excellent down to 100mph, but it became sluggish near the stall at 68mph in landing configuration. Approaches, overshoots and landings showed that this big aeroplane handled much like a Hurricane (and more docilely than a Spitfire), although it had less tendency to 'float' then either. A major bonus was its very wide undercarriage which made it surprisingly stable on rough ground and much less sensitive to crosswinds than a Spitfire.

So, as the flight ended, it became clear that this big ugly fighter was actually pleasant to fly — if only the pilot could stick his fingers in his ears and could see properly out of it.

From March until the end of June many opportunities arose to take part in the last phase of the Typhoon test programme, and early production Ias and Ibs were flown at Langley in a wide range of trials. Long and wearying low level sorties were flown in *R8220* with vibrograph recording of the vibration levels which were bothering both the authorities and the pilots; some of the latter claimed concern over the possible effects of the fatiguing vibrations on their marital prospects, resulting in many modifications to relieve the problem including improved balancing of propellers and the introduction of spring-mountings for the pilot's seat. Collectively these measures may have altered the vibrations experienced by the pilot, but in the end the writer could not recall any noticeable reduction — the Typhoon was always a rough aeroplane but, as time would show, a very useful one.

Hawker test pilots at Langley in 1943. From left to right, Lucas, Broad, Humble, Silk, Pegg, Hyams, author, unknown, Fox, unknown.

Chapter 5

Typhoons into battle

In 609 Squadron at Duxford during the summer of 1942 I had begun to feel that it was time to investigate other possible rôles for the Typhoon and as a start arranged for night trials leading, if successful, to moonlight operations against enemy activity within range of Duxford. The first of these was in *PR-F* on the night of 25 July and was successful. After a second trial on the 26th an operational patrol was flown on the 28th, and under GCI (Ground-Controlled Interception) a 'friendly' was identified without difficulty as a Wellington.

The Typhoon was clearly a stable and controllable aeroplane for night flying, and it seemed likely to give a good account of itself in gunnery, both air-to-air and air-to-ground — so a possible path for future investigation could be its use in day and night ground attack. A report was requested by and sent to the Air Ministry where it was received with interest and possibly some initial disbelief, and it was commented on by Philip Lucas, Hawker's Chief Test Pilot, in a letter of 1 August 1942. Lucas confirmed that the earlier activities on cockpit vision improvement were bearing fruit and that an improved windscreen and canopy were under development.

TO: S/Ldr G.L. Sinclair DFC
                   F.O.1 Air Ministry

FROM: F/Lt R.P. Beamont

SUBJECT: Suitability of Typhoon IB for Night flying/*PR-V* Serial *R7708*

DATE: 25/7/42

Night flying on the nights of 24 and 26 July
Full moon, 6/10 cloud, wind SW 25mph and 10/10 cloud, wind SW 5mph

Cockpit lighting

The three standard cockpit lights (port, starboard and compass) are quite useless as fitted at present though they can be improved and made usable by painting the bulbs red. However the range of illumination given at present by the port and starboard lights is insufficient, and the addition of two masked red lamps in the top left and right hand corners of the instrument panel is necessary.

Taxying

The view for taxying is comparable with that of the Hurricane and is therefore quite satisfactory. It has, however, become general practice to taxy rather fast in this aircraft and this should be avoided at night as the brakes, though good directionally, are not very positive for pulling up. The last minute cockpit check is very simple, as the engine instruments are well placed and the rudder bar, tail trim and flap position can be easily felt.

The complete absence of exhaust glow and sparks is a great asset.

Take-off

Again the exhaust glare is very conspicuous by its absence — a point which will be greatly appreciated by Hurricane and Spitfire night pilots. The take-off from Duxford aerodrome was found to be slightly difficult owing to the extreme roughness of the surface, and the aircraft could not be held in flying position for any length of time without being thrown into the air from some particularly uneven part. However the Macdonald flare-path could be seen clearly at all times and the take-off runs were sufficiently short to create complete confidence. On runways or a smooth grass surface the take-off would present no difficulties at all.

Handling in flight

All the instruments are well positioned, but the ASI and the rev counter cannot be seen without the additional lamps previously mentioned. For instrument flying it is necessary to lower the seat to the bottom position in order to see the Artificial Horizon. This is no disadvantage. On a number of older type Typhoons, curved perspex quarter panels were fitted to the wind shield. Night flying was carried out in an aircraft of this type, and this was a definite disadvantage as the distortion from these panels is of a high order, and at the same time there was a large amount of interior reflection from instrument lights and also from the moon when flying away from it.

None of these conditions were found when flying an aircraft with the now standard 'straight' glass quarter panels.

All normal manoeuvres were carried out including aerobatics, and semi half-rolls as might be used for following evasive tactics, and the aircraft was found to be if anything more pleasant to fly at night than a Hurricane.

Night vision

This appears to compare favourably with that of a Spitfire and slightly unfavourably with that of a Hurricane, but when cruising at 285 IAS with both windows down — a condition which is quite comfortable for the pilot — I was quite easily enabled to sight a Wellington at 1,000yd and close with it (with the moon behind it).

Again the complete absence of exhaust glare at any throttle setting was a great advantage. The forward vision will be greatly improved with the introduction of the 'clear view wind shield' now under development.

All night flying Typhoons should be fitted with the standard hood, as the blister hood with the mirror cuts out an important area of search vision.

Landing

Very straightforward and simple. The view is good even when making a low approach, and the approach may be made at 120 IAS W & F* down reducing to 100 IAS approximately 100yd before the glide path indicators (on the Macdonald system) at 30ft.

(With the tail down the flare path is easily seen and the aircraft can be held straight quite simply on the ground.)

* Wheels & Flaps.

General remarks

The Typhoon should prove satisfactory for GCI under moon conditions, and for 'Fighter Night', Searchlight 'Box' work etc. Under ideal conditions it is also very suitable for short range intrusion owing to its ability to reach the target area quickly, and to close rapidly with any EA sighted.

The overshooting bug should not be considered against it as speed can easily be lost when the pilot is prepared.

Clear dark night flying with the Typhoon would also be perfectly normal, but of doubtful practicability.

The Typhoon should *NEVER* be flown at night under conditions of rain, as the airstream peculiar to this aircraft causes the hood and windshield to become almost completely opaque even in daylight in the slightest rain shower.

R.P. Beamont
F/Lt

Flight Lieutenant R.P. Beamont, DFC
No 609 (WR) Squadron
Royal Air Force
DUXFORD
Cambs

1 August 1942

My dear Bee

Very many thanks indeed for your most interesting report on night flying and for your letter. It would be grand if you could get the first Hun at night. I am glad, too, that you think the machines could be operated satisfactorily in the dark.

Both 1 and 257 Squadrons have now received most of their machines and they seem highly delighted with them, which is very encouraging.

I sincerely hope, too, that the modified Clarke viscosity valves will solve the sleeve wear trouble which, after all, appears to be the only outstanding point.

With regard to the cockpit top, you will be glad to hear that very strong pressure is now being brought to bear to have a sliding hood fitted and to introduce the clear-view windscreen as quickly as possible, as even if the sliding hood is finally approved, it will be some time before you see it, as some considerable development work may be necessary.

Looking forward to seeing you soon,

Yours,

Philip Lucas

Subsequently on 2 February 1943, the writer flew the first installation of this new arrangement in experimental Typhoon serial *R8800* at Langley and, finding it a massive improvement over the original, recommended introduction as a new standard for fighter vision. This modifica-tion was to reach production in later series Typhoons in 1943–44 and in all production Tempests, but in the meantime in the summer of 1942 the squadrons were stuck with what they had, and they set about making the best possible use of them.

★   ★   ★

At Duxford on the morning of 18 August 1942 the pilots of the Typhoon Wing consisting of 266 (Rhodesian), 609 (WR Auxiliary) and 56 Squadrons were called to a briefing which, somewhat unusually, was first addressed by John Grandy* who commanded the Duxford sector. He told the briefing in his usual blunt and cheerful style that a major operation was about to begin which would take our forces back to France for the first time since our hurried withdrawal in May 1940. For some of us who had taken part in that battle and the subsequent Battle of Britain this was a tremendous moment, but he went on to say that in view of the prevailing technical problems with our new Typhoons, which were still suffering engine failures and tail breakages at the time, all he would do on this occasion was to tell us that we could go on this operation if we wanted to, but if we thought the Typhoon wasn't ready he would go along with that.

The Wing Leader, Dennis Gillam, then outlined the operations plan for the Duxford Wing to reinforce West Malling and from there 'sweep' behind Dieppe at 10,000ft to provide fighter cover over a major sea-borne attack on the harbour and coastal defences. There was no hesitation at all — the Wing would go to Dieppe! Grandy was clearly delighted and the rest of the day was a whirl of preparation and repolishing of windscreens, running engines, checking guns and going over the briefing plan. The Wing was, in fact, at the end of a drawn-out and frustrating introductory period with its new Typhoons, and was more than ready to have a go.

Early on the morning of the 19th the Typhoon Wing took off to sweep down the enemy coast from Dunkirk to Calais without result, before landing at West Malling. 609 Squadron, led by Paul Richey, took the opportunity for some close formation practice on the way back.

Malling was hot and dusty in the August sunshine and appeared to be almost submerged in fighters as the Typhoons taxied in past squadrons of Spitfires, Hurricane bombers and Beaufighters. Then, after a quick refuelling the pilots were back in the cockpits awaiting the green Very light which would signal 'start up'. This, when it came, resulted in an eruption of starter cartridge reports, smoke, exhaust flame and dust as 36

2,000hp Sabre engines fired. Taxying out over the dry grass airfield caused problems as the big three-bladed propellers churned dust and debris into the eyes of pilots straining to see through their cockpit side windows which were open until take-off to try and avoid excessive heat. Then the leader's Section was away with the squadrons following Section by Section in a rising pall of dust.

With no preliminary circuit to close up the formation, the Wing leader set course at low level for Beachy Head with all 36 Typhoons closing to 'search formation' as they crossed out over the chalk cliffs with climb power, ignoring the enemy radar on this occasion and going directly up to 10,000ft. Immediately the VHF became noisy with the menacing sound of enemy radio interference and with spasmodic instructions and excited observations from other squadrons already in action.

Levelling over mid-Channel at 10,000ft, Dennis Gillam leading the Wing with 56 Squadron maintained high power until the Typhoons were indicating 300mph for fast target penetration, and then the enemy coast was in sight through a layer of broken cumulus cloud at about 2–4,000ft. Turning west from the Somme estuary, the three Typhoon squadrons made an impressive sight with their blunt nose radiators and aggressive overall shape; then the action began.

Confused radio chatter suggested enemy aircraft inland somewhere. Almost simultaneously some unidentified aircraft were seen below momentarily through gaps in the cloud, and then the harbour and sea front of Dieppe. It was now ringed in smoke and fires with white tracks offshore of weaving naval vessels and assault craft and the unmistakable splashes of sticks of bombs.

The Typhoons swept on over Dieppe with no immediate target in sight, although at some point a section of 266 Squadron broke away and dived after some Dorniers, claiming 'probables'; and Gillam led the Wing in a long diving sweep at 400mph round behind Dieppe and down through the broken cloud layer to look for activity. Some pilots reported a fleeting glimpse of some '190s or '109s (or Spitfires) before they disappeared into cloud, and then the rear section of 609 Squadron saw '190s in and out of cloud for long enough to attack them and claimed three damaged.

*Later Chief of the Air Staff and Governor of Gibraltar.

Soon the Wing was crossing out on its way back to Malling for a welcome cool drink while refuelling before setting off to do it again; but this time it was over total cloud cover and there were no enemy sightings. At the end of the day when the Wing landed back at Duxford in the quiet, warm dusk of the Cambridgeshire countryside, one Typhoon had been lost with engine failure and another shot down by a Spitfire. The Typhoons had claimed two 'probable' enemy aircraft victories and three damaged and had taken a very small part in a great and heroic raid.

The enemy may possibly have been as frightened by the Typhoons as we were at the time though one doubts it — but the day of the Typhoon was still to come. Meantime, this brief experience of major air combat conditions highlighted once again the total unsuitability of the Mk I Typhoon's cockpit, windscreen and canopy design, for air superiority fighting.

⋆   ⋆   ⋆

By October the Duxford Typhoon Wing had been disbanded and the squadrons dispersed for trial operations in other rôles such as home defence, coastal defence against 'tip and run' raiders; and later for dive- and low-level bombing for which a new squadron was formed in 1943 under Squadron Leader Denis Crowley Milling. This unit's aircraft were fitted with under-wing bomb racks for 500 and 1,000lb bombs and had a modified gun/bombing sight.

Now under the writer's command, 609 Squadron was moved in October 1942 to the most famous Spitfire sector station, Biggin Hill, where its reception was less than enthusiastic. In fact, after a short time in which the Typhoons had been restricted entirely to coastal patrols, when the writer asked the Wing Leader directly for the inclusion of 609 in the next Biggin Hill sweep, the answer was 'No, Biggin Hill is a Spitfire Wing and Typhoons aren't suitable'.

A request to 11 Group Headquarters resulted in an immediate move to Manston with a brief to 'investigate practical operational uses of the Typhoon within the limits imposed by [your] commitment to standing patrols of the coastline between Ramsgate and Dungeness in the hours of daylight'. This gave the writer the necessary opportunity and considerable local independence, and plans were made for offensive trial

operations to begin immediately.

On the first of these I flew *PR-G*, serial *R7752*, on 17 November on a moonlight 'Rhubarb' sortie to the Somme estuary, easily finding a train near Abbeville and stopping it in two attacks amid a great deal of steam and some harassment from flak and searchlights (See Appendix 3). On 13 December two trial daylight 'Rhubarbs' were flown to Amiens; the first encountered bird damage and the second found valid targets (Appendix 4). On 21 November a night 'Intruder' sortie had been flown in *PR-F* and three trains were attacked at Amiens and Abbeville marshalling yards through intense flak (Appendix 5). A second 'Intruder' that night with *PR-F* produced a train attacked at Poperinghe, and some keen return fire from an AA wagon behind the engine until it was silenced; and the month finished with a night 'Intruder' on the 22nd to the Somme area and an attack on another train at Abbeville (see Appendix 6).

This activity served two purposes: it confirmed my view that the Typhoon could be a potent and valuable ground-attack aircraft by both day and night, and it brought this view to the notice of the higher powers. Reports were requested and the writer was summoned to meetings at Group and Command headquarters where the overall future of the Typhoon was under review.

From the first practice gun attacks carried out on a wreck off Pegwell Bay near Manston it was obvious that forward vision through the heavy-framed windscreen structure would be a problem, particularly in bad weather, and this was emphasized in the moonlight attacks. Targets could be found and identified from about 1,000ft by moonlight through the open wind-down side windows, but when turning in to attack, the target disappeared behind the thick fore/aft windscreen members; then, if it was picked up in the thick armourglass front panel, it was frequently lost again when transferring past the GM2 gunsight brackets into the reflector. In addition, a low-contrast target could seldom be seen behind the bright 'ring and range bars' image of the gunsight. All of this was made significantly worse in haze or smoke at night, or in rain or mist in daytime.

Nothing could be done about the windscreen until the factory modification appeared on new aircraft, but I decided to experiment with improvement to the gunsight itself. With enthusiastic help from the squadron armourers, the gunsight on *R7752* was modified to remove the ring and range bars, leaving only the centre spot aiming point; this was a significant improvement when tried out in bad weather over the Pegwell Bay wrecks.

Next, the sight reflector glass and bracket were removed, and the sight itself was re-set to reflect directly on to the armourglass windscreen. At full brilliance this resulted — as expected — in some double images, but these were effectively reduced when the brilliance was set down to the low level relevant to the target lighting conditions. When it was tested by moonlight with the aiming spot brilliance set at the minimum practical level, the overall effect was striking.

These two measures had so improved the Typhoon's forward vision that ground attacks in night or low cloud conditions could now be made with the confidence of holding the target once it had been acquired; this was soon put to the test over France in further train attacks with excellent results. Although all-round vision was still inadequate for day combat, the limited ground-attack vision was now sufficient and the writer ordered all 609 Squadron aircraft gunsights to be modified. This was done 'because of operational necessity' without Headquarters armament branch authorization, and when these worthies heard about it there followed a rising crescendo of abrupt instructions to remove the modifications.

However, 609 found them ideal and continued to use them with success throughout the long winter of 1942–43; and the 'direct reflection' modification subsequently received the accolade of reluctant official approval when introduced, in conjunction with specially selected 'Grade A' armourglass, as standard fit for Tempest V production.

In December 609 took off! On a rising tempo of enthusiasm pilots completed the special night training laid down, and day 'Rhubarbs' and night 'Intruders' became normal routine. The writer flew nine offensive sorties in *PR-G* — mostly at

Left *The author with* PR-G.

Below *Typhoon Ib of 609 Squadron — the CO's aircraft.*

night — and in the last on 23 December damaged three trains, bringing the total to twelve since 17 November. In this period the squadron attacked 25 trains, destroyed four low-flying Fw 190 raiders and damaged others. The Typhoon was proving a fast and capable air defence fighter at low level, and an accurate and effective gun platform for its 20mm cannon on ground targets.

At a formal meeting at the Bentley Priory headquarters of Fighter Command in early 1943, with the Commander-in-Chief in the chair, a last attempt was made (mainly by the engineering branch and a Spitfire lobby) to cancel the Typhoon in favour of buying an American heavy fighter for ground attack. However, largely on the evidence of the 609 findings and with support from the experienced Belgian CO of No 3 Squadron, Squadron Leader de Soomer, the Typhoon survived and went on to become the main ground attack weapon of the RAF for the invasion of Europe in 1944.

Meanwhile, 609 Squadron's task had only just begun and the months to June were spent actively on the offensive, with day and night low level attacks interspersed with the continued coastal patrols — which were soon extended from the original 'five miles out' to within five miles of the French coast. A particularly successful operation occurred on 4 April 1943 (See Appendix 7).

A good measure of success was achieved with few losses, the majority still due to engine failure which was generally fatal if it occurred over the sea and the pilot tried to ditch; but the Air Sea Rescue Service made some remarkable recoveries of Typhoon pilots who had baled out.

Towards the end of this period 609 began bombing trials carrying 500lb inert bombs on the two underwing racks. The writer was puzzled after the first experimental 'shallow bombing' attacks against a small wrecked ship on the Goodwin Sands, because no splashes were visible in the sea to show where the bombs had landed. A second sortie had the same result, but after the last bomb a puff of debris from the wreck showed where this concrete bomb (and apparently all the others) had gone straight into the side of the target ship, with of course no explosion to reveal this more clearly! This was another indication of the excellence and accuracy of the Typhoon in low attack rôles, and it was in this area that Crowley Milling's 181 Squadron 'Bomb-phoons' set high standards in their attacks on targets in France in late 1943, leading to the concentrated and dangerous work of bombing the 'Noball' V-1 launching sites in 1944, with the rest of the rapidly built-up bomber and rocket Typhoon force in 2nd TAF.

Throughout 1943 the engine and airframe reliability of the Typhoon continued to improve, and by the end of the year the cause of many fatal tail failures had been traced to fatigue fractures of the elevator mass-balance brackets, and was easily cured. Meanwhile, 609 and increasing numbers of new Typhoon squadrons extended their activities in very successful deep-penetration 'Ranger' operations, and destroyed many enemy aircraft around or on their base airfields in France, Belgium and Holland.

The writer was posted back to Hawkers at the end of June to take part in the investigation of the tail breakages, and to join the programme for

Left *Pilot Officer Skett's Typhoon after a 'Rhubarb' low attack operation from Manston on 2 March 1943.*

Right *The author in PR-G as CO of 609 Squadron, Manston 1942–43.*

Right *The Air Minister visits 609 Typhoon Squadron at Manston. From left to right, Group Captain Desmond Sheen, Sir Archibald Sinclair and the author.*

No 609 Squadron pilots at Manston. From left to right, Skett, Spallin, two unknowns, Haabjorn, Van Lierde, Evans, author, Blanco, Cameron, Raw, Wells, Stark, Payne, Polek and Lallemande.

clearance of the Typhoon's much improved successor, the Tempest, into service in time for the coming invasion of Europe. This aircraft, when it reached the squadrons in March 1944, incorporated all of the Typhoon's improved vision modifications and set undoubtedly the highest standard of combat and attack vision of any fighter of its time.

During the remainder of 1943 and early 1944 the build-up of the Typhoon ground-attack force continued, and by the invasion day of Operation 'Overlord' ten squadrons were in action in close support of our armies. They were under the brilliant leadership of Wing Leaders Denis

Gillam, Johnny Baldwin, Walter Dring, Desmond Scott, Eric Haabjoern, Charles Green and others, and built up a legendary reputation of accuracy and courage in the battles for Europe. Frequently their results were so devastating that they directly affected the course of the land battle. This was readily admitted by the enemy, particularly after the massive destruction of armour at Mortain and Falaise during the enemy retreat from the bridge-head at Caen.

From its 1938 specification as a 'bomber-destroyer' the Typhoon had finally evolved and found its vital rôle as one of the best ground-attack fighters of World War 2.

Chapter 6
Test flying the Tempest...and into battle

The winter of 1943 had seen continuous activity by the Typhoons of 609 Squadron across the Straits of Dover from Manston, and in these actions the Typhoon had proved to be a versatile and rugged aircraft despite its unbeautiful appearance and its early bad reputation for engine unreliability and structural failures. It was with investigation of the latter problem that the author became involved together with Hawker test pilot Bill Humble, at the Langley factory in the summer of 1943. This test programme had followed the loss of a number of Typhoons and their pilots in high-speed dives, including Hawker's experimental test pilot Ken Seth-Smith who had carried out a major part of the early testing of the Typhoon and Tornado prototypes with chief test pilot Philip Lucas.

The Typhoons had proved fast and effective against Fw 190 'tip-and-run raiders' around the Channel coast at low level and in combats up to 20,000ft; but above that their manoeuvrability fell away in comparison with that of the '109s and '190s. Also, the high speed and good 'gun platform' stability of the Typhoon had proved

advantageous for ground-attack in wide-ranging armed reconnaissance operations over France, Belgium and Holland. But the early Typhoons had this one major disadvantage — visibility from the cockpit was so exceptionally bad for a fighter that in a combat mêlée the Typhoon pilot felt as if he was in blinkers — an unpleasant feeling with '109s around! The aircraft was also fuel-restricted to about $1\frac{1}{2}$ hours maximum. These and other criticisms had been fed back to the manufacturers, and by early 1943 the first prototype of a 'Typhoon 2' development had appeared at Langley. It was intended that the new and vastly improved windscreen and 'clear-view' one-piece Perspex canopy would replace the Typhoon's heavy-iron-to-glass ratio structure; that a new wing of improved thickness/chord ratio (10.5 per cent at the tip, 14.5 per cent at the root and maximum thickness at 37.5 per cent chord) with semi-elliptical plan-form would improve performance, and that increased underwing fuel tankage would provide about 25 per cent increase in range/endurance.

Now called 'Tempest' the first prototype,

HM595, *the first Tempest prototype, with new nose and wing but retaining the Typhoon cockpit and tail structure. Langley, 1943.*

HM595, made its first flight on 2 September 1942 with Philip Lucas at the controls. This was the Sabre-engined Mk V version which had the new wing and lengthened nose, but retained the Typhoon-style cockpit and tail unit. Its handling characteristics were soon seen to be an improvement.

Second in the series was Mk I prototype, *HM599*, flown on 24 February 1943 by Bill Humble. This had the new wing with leading-edge radiators in place of the big under-nose radiator 'bath' of the Typhoon; it still retained the Typhoon tail and cockpit, but both of these were modified to the new Tempest design later that year.

The author's first Tempest test flight was on 2 June 1943 at Langley in the sole Tempest I, *HM599*, and this was a revelation in the improvement of performance and rolling manoeuvrability. Two further flights on the 4th and 5th were on performance 'levels', and it was

apparent that this aircraft was at least 50mph faster than the Typhoon, with possibly more to come.

Prior to this I had evaluated a prototype of the new windscreen and one-piece sliding canopy development on an experimental Typhoon (*R8809*) on 2 February 1943 at Langley, in a dog-fight with the Centaurus-engined Tornado prototype flown by Seth-Smith. It was a revolution in fighter vision and strong recommendations were made for its adoption. This configuration eventually became standard on the Typhoon Series 2 and on all production marks of the Tempest, and was next fitted retrospectively to the Tempest I for further trials.

During the remainder of June 1943, *HM599* carried out intensive performance trials with Bill Humble and the author flying alternately, and these gave proof of the exciting potential of this aircraft to reach speeds in excess of the existing

Right *The new 'Tempest' wing planform.*

Above Left *The Tempest I experimental prototype at Langley in 1943.*

Left *The Tempest I modified with the clear-vision cockpit and showing the wing radiators.*

Left HM595 *with development fin for experimental testing.*

Below *The second production Tempest V with the final fin shape, revised cockpit vision and 'long' cannons. This was the first operational Tempest series.*

Bottom right *The first Tempest II prototype at Langley in 1943 showing the 'Typhoon' fin which was later modified to Tempest V standard.*

world speed record of 454mph which had been set by a special Messerschmitt in 1939. Reference books give the maximum speed achieved by '599 as 466mph at the maximum-power altitude, 24,000ft; but in the Langley experimental department it was believed that 470mph was exceeded on a number of occasions.

The large four-bladed propeller together with spreading the radiators along the wing leading-edge were found to have a de-stabilizing effect and directional damping was too low for good gun-aiming, so an increase in fin area became necessary. This was tried out as an interim modification on the Mk V, *HM595*, which the author flew on 7 June 1943 and confirmed that it

showed ideal qualities of directional 'stiffness'.

Neither of these prototypes yet had the improved vision and *JN729*, the first production Tempest V, was the first of the series with all the major modifications. This aircraft was flown by Bill Humble first on 21 June 1943, and it was to become the main test aircraft for final clearance into service of the Tempest V. I flew it on the following day and was immediately impressed with its general feeling of improved responsiveness and crispness over the Typhoon, but felt that rate of roll and aileron heaviness needed improvement. Vision from the cockpit was superb. This was the test aircraft for Hawker's new spring-tab aileron control system designed

by F.W. Page*, and in the next few weeks intensive trials were flown to optimize the spring-tab system, reverting at times to the original geared tabs for comparison. On one of these geared tabs flights in '729 on 21 September, the author encountered one of the main problem areas when, at near the dive limits at about 530mph IAS, violent aileron overbalance occurred and flicked the aircraft inverted.

By the end of September the spring-tabs had been fine-tuned to give high-rate roll without overbalance right up to the dive limit of 545mph IAS, and it was clear that with this high speed manoeuvrability coupled with superb all-round vision the Tempest was going to be a fighter to reckon with — but the time scale was short and the target of into-service in time for the invasion of France and the Low Countries which was expected to take place in the spring of 1944, was already less than six months away — and then another problem occurred.

The two prototypes had given no significant problems with the Sabre II and IV engine installation married to revised radiator systems, and the production Mk V series was expected to reproduce the satisfactory engineering characteristics of *HM595*. However, as the aileron testing on *JN729* began to reach the limiting dive speeds, full throttle climbs in summer temperatures to the necessary altitudes for starting the dives began to show a new defect — the radiator boiled!

* Until 1982 Chief Executive, Aircraft Group, British Aerospace.

Coolant temperature rising towards limits was noted every time on a full throttle climb passing 15,000–16,000ft, and on 4 August *JN729* went off the limit and boiled when the author was deliberately continuing at full throttle to 17,000ft. A throttled-back descent soon cooled it and no damage was done, and the engineers worked on the problem. It was established that the system was 'to drawing' and was clean and free of swarf or dirt, and no positive defect was found; but on the assumption that if the previous radiator system on the prototype had been marginally adequate then only a small improvement in cooling capacity should prove effective, a 'swan-neck' modification was tried on '729 which modestly increased the length of pipe run from the header-tank to the radiator itself. On 15 September I flew this modification on a full throttle/fine pitch climb right to the 100fpm ceiling at 37,000ft without exceeding the radiator limits.

The remainder of 1943 was an intensive period at Langley with forty to fifty experimental test flights per pilot/month as the norm. In this the final sorting of the Tempest V was interspersed with further Typhoon tail-failure testing which included simulating engine failure by cutting the ignition switches from full throttle at 500mph in vertical dives to achieve near design-limit yawing factors; and also early tests of the prototype Tempest II, *LA602*, with the Centaurus IV 2,500hp radial engine.

The author's first flight in this aircraft was on 7 August and, although the power of the big engine

A Tempest V Series 2 with 'short' cannon on test from Langley with Bill Humble flying in 1944.

was appreciated, the large radial cowling restricted the view for taxying and caused a noticeable reduction in directional damping in all flight conditions. This was with the original Typhoon fin and it was intended that, when the production series Tempest fin was adopted, adequate gun-aiming stability would be obtained. In the event, when the second Mk II, *LA607*, flew in this configuration it was found to be still barely adequate directionally and not up to the excellent standard of the Mk V; but possibly because by the time the Mk II appeared in production the end of the war in Europe was in sight, further development was dropped. So although the Tempest II saw service in Germany and the Middle East in the immediate post-war years, its handling was never quite up to the crisp, taut directional standard of the Mk V

In the last months of 1943 the emphasis at Langley was on setting the Tempest V production standard, and *JN730, 731, 736* and *743* joined *JN729* in intensive test-flying to obtain 'CA Release' for service in early 1944. In this phase, with the emphasis on clearing the extreme corners of the flight envelope, *'729* was dived repeatedly to the 545mph V_{ne}* — an unusual number to read on an ASI in 1943.

Even at these speeds, in contrast to the noise, buffet, vibration and general commotion

---

* V_{ne} — Velocity never exceed, ie, the maximum speed an aircraft is designed to be flown at.

experienced in the Typhoon as it approached its 500mph limit, the Tempest remained smooth, buffet-free, stable and crisp in pitch and yaw and responsive and well-damped in roll. It just felt fast, efficient, undramatic and very good indeed.

In order to confirm that this was not just an isolated aspect, every opportunity was taken after the completion of the scheduled tasks to 'bounce' any targets that presented themselves such as the Typhoons on test from Langley and itinerant Spitfires. On one occasion a strange twin-boom jet was intercepted which turned out to be the prototype Vampire in the hands of Geoffrey de Havilland from Hatfield. Generally the pilots concerned would try to 'mix it' which gave good practical experience, and the way in which the Tempest V could intercept, out-manoeuvre and then track these evading targets accurately in the directly-reflected gunsight was proof positive. This fighter was going to be a winner.

Every opportunity was also taken to assess overall suitability for ground attack in as wide a range of adverse conditions as possible. Often using a grounded balloon of the Langley barrage as a target in turbulence, crosswinds, mist, rain, smog and sleet or snow, these tests showed conclusively that in addition to its excellent controllability and superb forward and all-round vision the Tempest was about to go into service with the best gun platform characteristics experienced on any fighter to that date.

In the event the first practical night trial was

JN751, *the author's personal Tempest V when Wing Commander/Flying of the first Tempest Wing, No 150, at Newchurch May-September 1944.*

carried out during Service work-up with the newly formed No 150 Tempest Wing, when *JN738* was flown by the author from Hornchurch to Bradwell Bay on the night of 4 March 1944; and after two further night flights with *JN738* which included aerobatics and simulated ground attacks (by moonlight), No 3 Squadron was instructed to add night training to its syllabus. This culminated in a full squadron night formation from Bradwell Bay on 26 April led by the author in *JN751*.

This activity caused observations of 'they must be mad' from the other day-fighters at Bradwell (sentiments probably shared by some members of No 3 Squadron!); but excellent suitability for night flying had been confirmed and these experiences subsequently served the Tempest Wing well on D-Day and other occasions in the summer of 1944 when operating on fighter sweeps and against interdiction targets across the Channel, as well as in all-weather day and night operations against V-1 flying bombs.

So, by the end of 1943 the team at Langley had established a level of confidence and enthusiasm for the Tempest V which was justified by subsequent events. The author delivered *JN731* to Boscombe Down on 22 October for the first official trial and by January 1944, with the satisfactory completion of handling and engineering tests with underwing drop tanks on *JN730*, the task was virtually complete although

Boscombe had some reservations on aspects of engineering detail which delayed the commencement of issue to the squadrons until early March 1944.

Meantime I had been charged with the interesting job of flying all the latest available fighters for comparison with the Tempest. These had included a Griffon Spitfire XII at Manston on 4 May 1943; a Spitfire VIII with a prototype clear-view canopy at Farnborough on 19 July; a P-51 Mustang I at Cranfield on 9 February 1944; a Spitfire XIV at Hullavington on 15 February 1944 and, most interesting of all, the first captured Fw 190 at Farnborough on 13 September 1943. This fascinating experience resulted in the happy conclusion that while all these fine aircraft had excellent characteristics and performance (especially the Fw 190), none were as good all-round as the Tempest and none could match the Tempest's speed below 10,000ft or its dive limit, still with excellent roll-rate remaining, of 545mph IAS.

Hans Werner Lerche in his book *Luftwaffe Test Pilot* speaks very highly of his flights in a captured Tempest V of 1945: 'There was no doubt about this one, the Tempest was an impressive high powered aeroplane by any standards — the improvement in performance and aerodynamic characteristics [over the Typhoon] was stunning'.

This was one of the few statements to come out

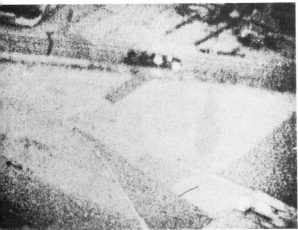

Frames from JN751's gun camera showing attacks on trains in northern France on 22 May 1944 during the 'softening up' period prior to D-Day.

of Germany in that period with which one could agree! Lerche also goes on to say that by his measurements the Tempest V was faster than the P-51D and that only the Me 262 jet fighter was its superior in climb and maximum speed.

All of this was already apparent to the team at Langley, and it was on a note of considerable enthusiasm that I flew a last Tempest test flight for Hawkers in *JN730* on 17 February 1944 before leaving Langley to rejoin Fighter Command to form the first operational Tempest unit, No 150 Wing of 85 Group, initially at Castle Camps and finally in the 11 Group fighting area at Newchurch on Dungeness for an exciting summer which included the D-Day operations*, the V-1 battle, wide-ranging ground attacks and long-range daylight bomber escorts to Germany. But it was in the battle against the V-1 Flying Bomb that the Tempest made its greatest single contribution at a crucial stage of the war in 1944.

By mid-June the Allied armies had established a strong foothold in Normandy, but had not reached the critical point of break-out from the beach-head area when Hitler was able to launch as a major diversion his massive attack with the V-1 weapon on London. The first flying bombs appeared on the night of 14 June, and within a few days launchings had reached about fifty in every 24 hours.

It was very soon seen that the outdated equipment of AA Command and their deployment in a defensive ring round outer London, was incapable of achieving an adequate success rate against this new and escalating threat — the guns were shooting down very few V-1s indeed. In general the air defences were more effective with large numbers of fighters of all types trying to intercept by day, and the fast Mosquitoes by night. But Spitfires V and IX, P-47 Thunderbolts, Typhoons and standard P-51 Mustangs proved to have barely enough speed to catch these fast targets, and their unco-ordinated ranging all over the skies of Kent and Sussex soon became counter-productive as they interfered with the work of the fastest fighters.

With the exception of the faster Spitfire XIIs and XIVs, some squadrons of Mustangs with specially uprated engines and the Tempest Wing, all the other squadrons had to be

* See Appendix 8.

Right *A V-1 flying bomb exploding under Tempest cannon fire over Kent in June 1944.*

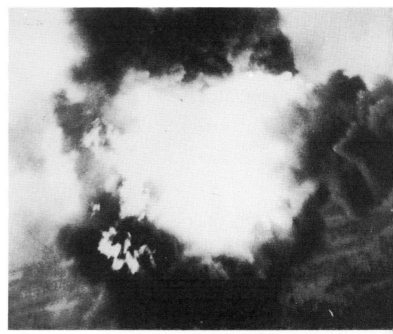

Below right *The author as Wing leader of 150 Tempest Wing in 1944.*

Below left *Bob Moore of No 3 Squadron who, with the author, accounted for the first enemy aircraft shot down by Tempests — three Me 109G-6s over Rouen on 8 June 1944.*

Left *Pilots of 122 Tempest Wing at Volkel, Holland, in October 1944, watched by young Dutch labourers.*

Right *The author forms the first Wing of Tempest IIs, Chilbolton, September 1945.*

withdrawn from the battle to leave uncluttered airspace for the small number of what now became specialist intercept squadrons. Chief of these in success rate by a large margin were Nos 3 and 486 Squadrons of No 85 Group flying Tempest Vs from No 150 Wing Newchurch, and these Squadrons were reinforced in July when new Tempests were rushed from the manufacturer to replace the Spitfire Vs of No 56 Squadron at Newchurch, and later No 501 Squadron at Manston.

It was immediately found that the Tempests could overtake the V-1s relatively easily (being 30–40mph faster than the best Spitfires and Mustangs at low altitude), and that with the Tempest's high quality gun-aiming stability the very small target presented by the V-1 was not a major problem. The Newchurch Wing's successes were immediate and sustained, pilots sometimes shooting down three each in one day; and the Tempests destroyed 600 flying bombs in the first full month of the battle during which time the whole of AA Command managed only 261, and all the fighters (together with the Tempests) 925.

A total of 1,691 V-1s reached greater London in the period, a figure that would have been increased by more than one third in the absence of the Tempests' vital contribution. The Press of the time were loud in their praise of the Tempests, but there it ended and no formal recognition was ever made of the tremendously effective and sustained efforts of all personnel of the Newchurch Wing in the defence of London in those first critical weeks.

There was some Service acknowledgement of these activities however, when two pilots from the Wing were summoned at very short notice to a 'Field Investiture' parade at RAF Blackbushe in July to be decorated with 'Immediate Awards' by King George. Normal citations were never received for these decorations, and the *London Gazette* briefly recorded that they were for general efficiency in operations with no mention of the V-1 battle.

Meantime, in August AA Command was able to redeploy en masse to the south coast with the latest technology equipment from the USA, which included radar gun-aiming and proximity-fuzed shells. In these circumstances they

immediately began to achieve a higher destruction rate, and by the end of August the fighters were released back to their normal duties. But despite the late success of the AA guns, the final score in September when the Army overran the launching sites in France and Belgium read 1,772 V-1s to the fighters and 1,460 to the guns; a total, including 231 by the balloons, of 51.5 per cent of all sightings.

It had become apparent that there was some central policy of giving over-fulsome credit to the AA guns for this defensive action, credit which they did not begin to earn until the second half of the battle; but it was not until many years later that the facts emerged. Prime Minister Churchill is recorded as having taken a strong view in the first weeks of the V-1 attack that this was a long-awaited opportunity to give some credit to AA Command in order to bolster their apparently flagging morale, and that no credit should be given to the RAF whatever happened!

As quoted in *Hitler's Rockets**, a memo from Churchill in March 1945 to the Chiefs of Staff read: 'You have no grounds to claim the RAF frustrated the attacks by the V weapons. . .so far as the flying bombs were concerned the RAF took their part, but in my opinion their efforts rank definitely below that of the A.A. artillery and still further below that of the army. . .I thought it a pity to mar the glories of the Battle of Britain by trying to claim overweening credit in this business of the V weapons.'*

To those who took part in both operations there was of course no comparison and no wish to make one; but there can be no doubt that history should record that London was spared a much heavier attack in June and July 1944 by the resolution, skills and sustained and desperate hard graft of all ranks of the RAF Newchurch Tempest Wing.

Ultimately the Tempests joined 2nd TAF in Holland in October 1944 for the battle for Germany†, and their successes were remarkable and sustained until VE-Day. The Tempest had arrived.

* Norman Longmate/Hutchinson, 1985.

* See Appendix 9.
† See Appendix 10.

Chapter 7

Meteor compressibility

Spring 1946 marked a new threshold in high speed flight.

Throughout the war years of 1939–45 the performance of military aircraft had increased progressively in relation to the rate of development of piston engines which advanced from around 1,000hp at the end of the 1930s to 2,500hp in 1945, with 3,000hp on the drawing boards for development of some of the big twin-row radials.

Of the inline engines, the massive Napier Sabre 24-cylinder H-section engine had survived its early near-catastrophic unreliability to become a formidable 2,000hp-plus power plant for the successful Typhoons and Tempests in the final great battles over Europe in 1944–45. Further stretch up to 3,000hp and more was envisaged, but with the end of hostilities the whole Sabre programme was discontinued on the grounds of cost and complexity, giving way to the rapidly emerging gas turbine jet engines.

This new power source was evolving on two lines, the rather bulky centrifugal-flow principle and the smaller cross-section axial-flow configuration. While the former had powered the first British jet aircraft, the Gloster E.28/39, the Meteor and the de Havilland Vampire, the emphasis by 1945 was already changing towards the enormous potential of the axial-flow engine, while the performance of the early Meteors had been increased by nearly 100mph with the introduction of Rolls-Royce Derwent 5 centrifugal engines for the Mk IV. In the autumn of that year Meteor IV serial *EE455* had set a new world air speed record at 606mph flown in its high speed trials by Group Captain W.P. Wilson of Farnborough and by Eric Greenwood, Gloster's chief test pilot; and still more speed was anticipated.

However, during the flight test programme at Gloster's experimental base at Moreton Valence a new limitation to level speed performance became apparent in 1945. Since the early testing of the Typhoons at Hawker's Langley factory in 1942, test pilots at the fighter factories and at Farnborough had become progressively more aware of the severe buffet and ultimate loss of lateral and longitudinal control which occurred in steep dives from high altitude with all the 400mph-plus fighters of the period. The arrival of the aerodynamically cleaner jets had not improved these matters significantly.

The propeller-fighters were becoming uncontrollable in dives at speeds approximating to 70–75 per cent of the speed of sound, but the significance of this was not immediately appreciated. Then the more powerful jets proved to be still disappointingly limited; for example, problems began at around Mach 0.74 in both the Vampire and the early Meteors, ie, slower than the Mach 0.76 recorded by Frank Murphy in a Tempest on test at Langley in 1944.

Much improved fineness-ratio nacelles for the Derwent 5 engined Meteor IV resulted in a further small increase in usable Mach number; and in an intensive series of dives to the out-of-control condition in March-April 1946 from Moreton Valence, mainly in *EE455*, the author found that Mach 0.79 was the new boundary of reasonable control.

By Mach 0.83–0.84 there was powerful pitch-down with no response to elevator, and the consequent dive had to be ridden down in violent buffeting until passing about 15,000ft where the nose began to rise slowly under continued heavy pull-force as the Mach number reduced with loss of altitude. This was a finite limitation which no Meteor IV was going to exceed operationally for

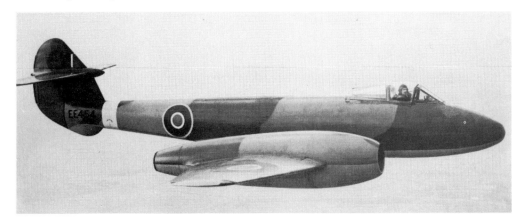

any practical purpose — but it was restricting only in the dive as the level thrust/drag performance maximum of about Mach 0.78 at altitude could be reached without serious control trouble, although buffet and the beginnings of compressibility trim changes were in evidence.

The margins were small however, and squadron pilots would now have to be trained on the technique for descents keeping clear of 'compressibility'.

At about this time notification was received of the RAF's intention to make a new attack on their own world speed record, and a special Meteor IV with the new clipped wing-tips was to be prepared with a spare aircraft, and tested to at least 10mph in excess of the existing record plus as great a safety margin as proved practical. It fell to the author to conduct these trials from Moreton Valence in July, but first Meteor Mk IV *EE455* was taken to Boscombe Down for airspeed indicator calibration tests. These were carried out

on 12 June 1946 with a Farnborough-supplied barograph installed, and the Meteor was flown past kine-theodolites mounted on highpoints on hangars and the headquarters building at about 60ft above ground. This provided some quite exhilarating flying as the progressive high speed runs, starting at 557mph IAS, reached the maximum found practical in these conditions at 580mph.

When corrected a massive position-error of +17mph was established; this meant that the fastest run had been only 9mph short of the existing record. To obtain the true speed of 616mph-plus required for a new record, an indicated speed of 600mph would need to be achieved as an average of one run in each direction on the day.

Back at Moreton Valence *EE549* with uprated Derwent 5 engines was cleared in stages to 595mph IAS at 1,000ft and then progressively lower reaching 605mph at 700ft. At these speeds

Above *Meteor IV, EE454, flown by Eric Greenwood, Gloster Aircraft's chief test pilot. Moreton Valence, 1945. This was one of two aircraft prepared in 1945 for the high speed trials.*

Right *The author in EE454 with strengthened canopy for the 1946 high speed trials.*

A Meteor T 7 over the Aust Ferry area of the low-level compressibility incident.

the noise level was impressive and the controls were noticeably stiffening; but response on all three axes was adequate and the decision was taken firstly to set up 605mph at 500ft and then, if practicable, take it down in a shallow descent at full power to reach an absolute thrust/drag maximum at 100ft above the Severn estuary in the over-water conditions specified for the RAF attempt which was eventually to be made off Littlehampton.

All these tests were ambient temperature sensitive, being at the thrust/drag boundary, and to achieve the highest IAS at the lowest Mach drag a hot day was needed. On 9 July this occurred with a Mct temperature of 27°C, and *EE549* was dived down the Severn over the Aust ferry to 595mph IAS at 200ft to assess turbulence. Conditions were dead calm with good visibility in bright sunshine, and so with a final tightening of harness straps and a health-check of engine instruments the Meteor was pulled up in a starboard turn over the Welsh bank of the Severn and rolled back south-west to line up over Aust and down the centre of the river towards Avonmouth with throttles wide open.

At 500ft with indicated speed at 600 mph and increasing, a final elevator trim adjustment was made and then the stick was eased back passing 200ft at 608mph IAS as the water began to look very close. Then it happened.

With a noticeable tuck-down the nose dropped and an adrenalin-inspired two-handed pull on the stick did not achieve the urgently needed response. With no chance to look again at the airspeed which was still increasing, the water was now a flashing blur immediately below and this was 'crisis corner'. In the seconds before what looked like imminent impact it was quite clear what was happening — this was 'compressibility' at sea level!

Knowledge that throttling back would only increase the nose-down moment left nothing else to do but pull hard with both hands and hope — and then, gradually, the nose began to rise and the Meteor flew clear. It had been a close thing indeed and on the way back to Moreton Valence, sweating from the heat of the high-speed run and the physical effort of the pull-out and a heightened adrenalin level, two things became clear.

Compressibility could be reached in this Meteor IV in only a shallow descent at low altitude and this would have to be avoided in future; furthermore, whatever true speed came out of the correction of this test point, in no way would this aircraft fly faster than that!

In the event the flight test engineers found that the corrected maximum true speed was 632mph,

The high-altitude trials Meteor IV at Warton in 1948, with Bill Eaves pre-flighting the cockpit.

and when Gloster's publicity department heard they immediately leaked it to the Press with results which were unfortunate and embarrassing because it had not been an official record, and also because there was no way in which the RAF could set as high a figure in their forthcoming trial — which would have to be carried out within safety limits recommended and approved by the Company.

EE549 was delivered to Tangmere in early August with a formal V_{ne} of 600mph IAS which, corrected, would give 614–618mph TAS (True Air Speed) depending on the temperature of the day. When Group Captain Teddy Donaldson skilfully broke the record for Britain again off Littlehampton in September, it was at 616mph TAS.

The record attempt clearance trials had the valuable effect of contributing further to the knowledge of the flight envelope boundary of the Meteor IV, and it was now possible to plot the absolute limits of control in indicated Mach number at close height intervals from sea level to 35,000ft. Above this the g-stall/shock-stall boundaries closed sharply towards each other with increase in altitude, but although it was soon realized that this would impose much more severe limitations on practical interception operations than implied by the makers' quoted

'operational ceiling 45,000ft', the actual boundaries had not been plotted.

Later, in 1947–48, English Electric at Warton carried out a special contract trial with Meteor IV serial *EE545* to explore and establish these limits in this remaining corner of the flight envelope from 35,000 to 45,000ft. In these trials from Warton together with the previous Moreton Valence tests, evidence had been obtained by the end of 1947 of more than sixty dives in Meteor IVs into the shock-stall, many of which resulted in delay in recovery to below 15,000ft before regaining level flight. After most of the extended climbs to absolute practical ceiling around 47,000ft before starting the dives, the resultant cold soak caused almost total opacity of the windscreen panels and canopy during the final descents to base when the moist, warm air lower down instantly iced over the outsides of the glass and frosted over the inner surfaces, blocking nearly all view. Then, in the absence of de-icing or adequately functioning de-misting systems, there was nothing for it but to accelerate (with the low remaining fuel) above 450kt IAS in order that the 'ram' temperature rise should begin to disperse the ice and mist. Sometimes this was only effective over a very small area of glass, and it was then something of a marginal problem to find the runway in the absence of any form of approach aid, and keep it in sight until touching down with the last remaining fuel.

In many ways this was a trial carried out to or beyond the conventional limits of safety, and at the time the Meteor IV was probably the first type to have its absolute limits of compressibility plotted so completely from sea level to operating ceiling; but it was a programme typical of the probing more or less into the unknown which characterized compressibility investigation and testing in those years.

Scientists thought they knew what was happening to airflow around airframes at 80 per cent of the speed of sound and what would happen at 100 per cent, but test pilots were not quite convinced as they continued to fall out of the sky in unsuitable aeroplanes with the maximum of buffeting commotion, violent trim changes and unresponsive controls. As a rhyme, circulated from Gloster's pilots' office to the design office at Bentham, put it:

'Sing a song of shock-stall, words by Ernest Mach

Four and twenty slide-rules shuffling in the dark...!'

But there was already a glimpse of light in the tunnel on the other side of the Atlantic. In 1947 Chuck Yeager flew the experimental rocket motor powered Bell X-1 to a level speed of Mach 1.05 in conditions of reasonable control, and in spring of the following year George Welsh dived the North American XP-86 Sabre fighter prototype to Mach 1 and recovered easily with conventional use of the controls. Practical supersonic flight was beginning to look possible, but there were some years and problems ahead and more lives to be lost before the North American Super Sabre, the Dassault Super Mystère and the English Electric P.1 ushered in the true supersonic era of the 1950s.

★   ★   ★

The years immediately following World War 2 were of major significance in the world of aviation. At the very moment of the expected massive run-down of industrial effort following the inevitable cutback of aircraft contracts at the end of hostilities, two new factors emerged which changed the course of events. They could not be ignored and together they ensured that the virtual cessation of military aircraft research, development and production so much desired by many politicians at the time, would not take place. These factors were the 'Cold War' and 'supersonics'.

The Russians continued their unwavering policy of hostility towards the West which contained the implied threat of expansionism wherever it suited their 'self-defence' posture, and which had recharged the international political atmosphere to high tension by the time of the Berlin Airlift. This led to the West hastily re-arming with new straight-winged jet fighters to replace the many thousands of Spitfires, Mustangs, Thunderbolts and Tempests still equipping their air forces.

The first jets in service were about 100mph faster than their propeller predecessors but they were less operationally flexible, being of shorter range and endurance and less manoeuvrable, and they were very costly. They were also almost immediately seen to be obsolescent when their ability to penetrate the 'compressibility barrier' showed disappointingly little improvement over the best of the propeller fighters. Talk began of 'supersonics' being essential for the next generation of military aircraft.

Scientific theory suggested that the 'compressibility barrier' could be overcome, and that once past it there would be no obstacle to further performance stretch until reaching a 'thermal' barrier at around Mach 2 to 2.5. This was akin to science-fiction for that period, and theory was not supported by factual evidence as the fastest new fighters were still found to be uncontrollable when dived to speeds in excess of 75–80 per cent of the speed of sound, with variations within this range depending on the type. Only one relevant common factor was firmly established — all existing high performance aeroplanes experienced a positive limit in 'compressibility' through which they could not penetrate in controlled flight.

It was against this background in 1945 that the Americans began a positive approach to supersonics with parallel programmes on the Bell X-1 rocket-powered research aircraft and the North American XP-86 swept-wing fighter prototype. Also in 1945, Miles Aircraft were engaged on a supersonic research prototype under Ministry contract. They were the only firm active in this field in the UK; the traditional fighter manufacturers were still concerned with developing their current straight-winged jet fighters.

In most of these first efforts however, the high drag of thick wings and large area side-intakes was to hold them firmly subsonic, and even when modified later with 35° swept wings they were still in trouble at transonic speeds.

At de Havilland the DH108 tailless research prototype had been lost at high speed over the Thames Estuary with Geoffrey de Havilland at the controls in 1946. A second prototype flown by John Derry was establishing that it could reach Mach 0.95 in control but with the effects of 'compressibility' in evidence. Later, in September 1948, Derry dived this aircraft to beyond Mach 1 at the tropopause where it became uncontrollable in pitch and roll until reaching a lower altitude and lower Mach number. This aircraft was also lost with its pilot, Squadron Leader Muller-Rowland, from RAE Farnborough in 1950.

In the middle of all this a government White Paper of 1947 announced no further interest in supersonic research. The Miles project was cancelled at the prototype stage, and it was stated 'that manned supersonic' flight would be too costly and dangerous (for the British) and that only a small programme of research into supersonic aerodynamics with models would be carried out at RAE. However the British had not, in fact, completely opted out. At the Preston works of English Electric, W.E.W. Petter's small and highly motivated team had the B3/45 Canberra project well on the way by 1947, and had by then taken the view that as there was no sign of the emergence of a new fighter design in this country which could deal with aircraft of the Canberra's predicted performance, who better than English Electric to do something about it!

So, totally ignoring government policy, English Electric decided to prepare a strong case for the need and practicability of supersonic performance for the next fighter, and at the same time to show precisely where the current crop of fighters and their developments would short-fall compared with the next generation of bomber and reconnaissance aircraft. Under the pretext of wishing to investigate the effects of high Mach numbers on stability, but in reality in order to obtain direct experience of the vital area above 40,000ft which they believed had not been thoroughly researched up to then by anyone, Teddy Petter obtained a Meteor IV on a Ministry contract for thirty hours of high altitude research.

This clipped wing aircraft, *EE545*, was collected by the author from Moreton Valence on 6 August 1947 and delivered to Warton's deserted airfield where it formed, with the support of experimental foreman Bill Eaves and a small servicing team, the basis of the first experimental test flying programme of post-war English Electric.

Facilities could have been described as less than rudimentary. The hangar (No 25) was unheated for the coming winter trials. There were no habitable offices. The runways and taxy tracks were heavily deteriorated and covered in loose stones. There were no radio or navigation aids, and 'air traffic control' consisted of foreman Eaves with an Aldis lamp!

In this atmosphere of operating on a shoestring backed by boundless enthusiasm and the Meteor's reliability, the trials made rapid progress hindered only by weather in the absence of radar or any form of homing device. VHF contact could only be maintained with Samlesbury ATC which also had no homing aids.

The flying soon became fascinating as limiting conditions were investigated progressively higher above 40,000ft. The controlled-flight gap between the stall and the compressibility 'shock-stall' closed to a point where above 45,000ft it was less than 40kt in 1g conditions. Any increase in g would of course rapidly narrow the gap; and it eventually became the 'norm' for these tests to, for example, set up Mach 0.79 at 45,000ft in the buffet and pitch-trim variations and then pull to the shock-stall at around 1.9g. At this point the Meteor would drop its nose sharply, rolling one way or the other with heavy buffeting, and would end up in a steepening dive with the Mach number increasing to 0.82–0.84 and the aircraft totally unresponsive to a two-handed pull on the stick. Eventually, after a height loss of 10,000ft or sometimes much more, it would recover as the Mach number dropped below 0.79 again.

All this was carried out in conditions of extreme cold in the cockpit, with the engines necessarily at full throttle resulting in rapidly lowering fuel gauges. There was the additional need, on almost every flight, for continuous attention to DR navigation complicated by the frequently unusual attitudes of the aeroplane, and with the certain prospect of complete misting and icing-up during the subsequent descent to base.

Forty-seven flights were made in the series up to 47,200ft, and mostly above 43,000ft. It was exhilarating stuff and it confirmed that no known fighter with Meteor characteristics, or even future aircraft with higher Mach capability up to 0.9 or so, were going to be able to carry out curve-of-pursuit attacks on aircraft of B3/45 (Canberra) performance above 40,000ft; and that if successful, the latter aircraft could be expected to enter service with at least a 10,000ft altitude advantage over anything else in sight. That it was seen as an inspiring situation is reflected in working papers, correspondence and reports between Teddy Petter and the relevant authorities in 1947–48.

After discussion of the results of the first phase tests, Petter circulated an internal memorandum:

'English Electric, Preston, 18 November 1947

'Following our recent conversation, and on further thought, I think it is very desirable that we should get in an interim report to the Ministry on the important discovery we are making of the high and low speed limitations of the Meteor at altitude. This, for the following reasons:

'(1) We are establishing that the Meteor is entirely useless for interceptions at heights exceeding 40,000ft. It is essential that this should be known by the Air Staff and a suitable fighter produced, if one is not already in hand, if there is to be any chance of dealing with bombers such as the B3/45.

'(2) It gives us a chance to demonstrate to ourselves and the Ministry that the B3/45 will be considerably better in regard to these limitations, both high and low speed.

'(3) It reinforces the case for getting on with the B35/46 design as proposed by us, rather than waiting for several years to obtain a few more knots, since the chances of intercepting, even at our cruising speed and altitude, seem to be pretty remote.

'(4) It demonstrates a valuable piece of research flying and allied thinking.'

This was followed by a note defining the detailed compressibility characteristics, to D.L. Ellis from the author on 2 December 1947:

'With reference to our conversation on the subject, the following is a brief description of the chain of events of compressibility as they affect the Meteor IV. To avoid confusion the Mach numbers quoted are "indicated".

'In normal flight, ie, level or dive at 1g, the following symptoms, which are common generally speaking to all altitudes, occur.

'(i) at Mach 0.75 there is a relatively high frequency airframe vibration in evidence, which provides a measure of warning, and which increases with Mach number.

'(ii) Mach 0.76. A tail down change of trim occurs and this can be, and is often, trimmed out.

'(iii) Mach 0.77. Regular pitching in evidence together with much vibration and increasing stick forces on all controls. Elevator losing effectiveness.

'(iv) Mach 0.785–0.79. Pitching changes to nose-down change of trim. Elevator ineffective though heavy and incapable of raising the nose, even with high stick forces. Considerable vibration and buffeting of ailerons.

'(v) Mach 0.82–0.83. Angle of dive increasing uncontrollably. Aileron buffeting increasing until wingtips appear to be stalling alternately. Little to no lateral control. It is of interest to note that there seems to be a slight decrease in the critical point (0.76 at 15,000ft) with increase in altitude, and that at this point the adequate margin of control ends. In this connection the dive brakes often prove to be very useful owing to their ability to be applied at high Mach number (as high as Mach 0.82) without adverse effect on control and with immediate effect on IAS and Mach number.'

Petter circulated an interim note to various authorities on 15 December 1947, containing for the first time (paragraph 5) a formal suggestion of a new approach to fighter design:

'Limitations on High Altitude Flying Flights on Meteor IV Aircraft

'1. A Meteor IV aircraft was recently loaned by the Ministry of Supply to the English Electric Company for the purpose of carrying out tests on stability at high Mach numbers and pressurisation problems at high altitudes. These tests are not yet complete, but some valuable data on flight at high altitude have been obtained, which it is thought are of sufficient importance to warrant a short interim note on the limitations experienced in flying at altitude at and over 40,000ft.

'These limitations are in no sense a reflection on the Meteor as a fighter aircraft for normal altitudes for which it was designed, but they do show that this, and similar machines, suffer from severe limitations when it comes to flying at very high altitudes; limitations which could only be overcome by fundamental alterations in wing loading on the one hand, and susceptibility to compressibility effects on the other.

'2. The attached graph shows the usable speed range empirically obtained, equivalent air speed being plotted against altitude. The boundary is taken as the speed which is thought to allow comfortable steady flight, but leaving us considerable margin for manoeuvre. A maximum acceleration of 2g has been assumed and the figures obtained in flight fall very closely on this curve for both high and low speed limits.

'The value of 2g was selected on the grounds that the accepted minimum approach speed for landing is $1.4V_s$* which allows the pilot a maximum of 1.96g. The physical effects of these boundaries as experienced by the pilot are discussed in the Appendix to this report.

'3. It will be seen that while there is a wide speed range available at low altitude, this rapidly narrows and theoretically reaches a point where one speed only can be used at about 46,000–48,000ft.

'The fact that the low speed bounding line bends over to the right instead of continuing vertically upwards is somewhat unexpected, but is explained by the fact that at the higher altitudes, the Mach number is reaching a figure which progressively limits the lift coefficient which can be used. The right-hand bounding line is quite simple and definitely established and corresponds to the Mach number at which compressibility buffeting is experienced at 2g. The estimated minimum drag speed is also shown on the graph, and it will be seen that this nearly coincides with the low speed boundary obtained in flight. This point was particularly noted in view of the differences of opinion which exist, and it was definitely established for this aeroplane and altitude that flight could be maintained for a considerable time without loss of

altitude or adjustment of the throttles, at this speed.

'4. Preliminary work on the B3/45 is yielding extremely interesting results and indicates that it will exceed the boundaries shown on the graph by a considerable margin. If sweep back, wing loading and wing section are suitably chosen as recently proposed for the B35/46, there should be a greater margin still. This work is the subject of another report to be issued shortly.

'5. Preliminary conclusions drawn from the foregoing are that an altogether different type of fighter will be necessary to provide defence against attacks from such machines as the B3/45 and B35/46, if such defence is possible at all.

'It would be necessary to give far more emphasis to speed, range and manoeuvrability, even at the expense of all-out level speed low down and, in particular, much lighter wing loadings on the one hand, and design for higher limiting Mach number on the other, will be necessary.'

This met with rapid responses from the Air Ministry and RAE Farnborough. The first, on 18 December, was from Air Vice Marshal John Boothman, Director of Technical Development at the Ministry:

'My dear Petter
'Thank you very much indeed for your letter dated 15 December 1947, to which you attached the notes discussing the results of the high flying tests which you have been making with the Meteor IV.

'These are of very great interest indeed, and I hope you do not mind, but I have made extracts and passed them on to Fighter Command because I think they will be invaluable. As you know, we are doing interception experiments at CFE in an endeavour to obtain some basic data for use in the future and so far these tests have been carried out at 35,000ft. It is obvious, however, that they will be running into a very different story when they go higher. A warning such as these notes will save them a lot of trouble.'

The second response, sent on the same day, was from M.B. Morgan, Superintendent of the Aero Flight Section at RAE Farnborough:

'Dear Petter
'Many thanks for the notes enclosed with your letter of 15 December 1947. The results obtained are of great interest to us, and we would welcome

---

*V_s — Velocity stall, ie, stalling speed.

being kept in close touch with the experiments.

'I feel that you are doing a first class piece of exploratory work, and the pilot in particular deserves congratulations for the able way in which he is tackling a very tricky job. I am sorry I was unavoidably away from the RAE when he recently visited us.'

Early in January 1948 Petter responded to the Director of Technical Development, Ministry of Supply, and referred to a possible future research contract based on the current Warton thinking:

'High Altitude Flying

'Very many thanks for your interesting and appreciative letter of 31 December 1947, on this subject. I am sure there is some further important practical and theoretical work to do which may have a big influence on future designs, and I am therefore very pleased to note that we are likely to get a research contract to continue in this field, and I shall look forward to attending the meeting you are going to call to discuss these problems.

'We have had discussions with Boscombe on two occasions including one yesterday with the Chief Technical Superintendent and the Superintendents of all the main Departments who visited us. The engine aspects in particular are being discussed today between our people and Rolls-Royce at Hucknall. I think the only reason that we placed less emphasis on the engine difficulties than did Boscombe was that we were not, at the time, concerned with the effect of these on operational flying, although in fact they are prohibitive, and we therefore accepted them and concentrated on the flying side. Nevertheless

General arrangement drawing of the Warton proposal for Air Ministry specification F23/49 (British Aerospace).

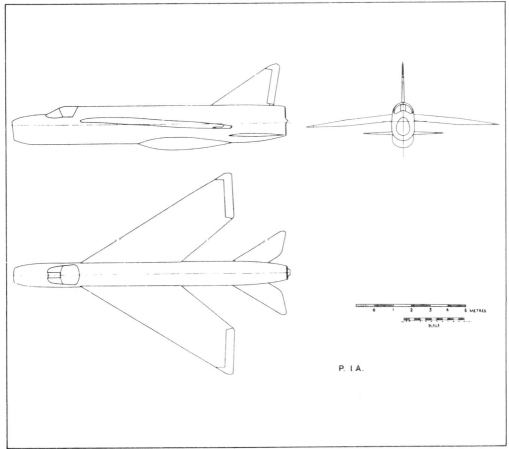

there were, on some occasions, unpleasant happenings.

'So far as pilot's safety goes, we have in general kept to 44,000ft or less, ie, the height at which our particular pilot, Wing Commander Beamont, is capable of carrying on for reasonable periods in event of pressure cabin failure. . .he has been checked in the pressure chamber at Farnborough for this. On one or two occasions he has been up to 47,000ft and we hope to do some more of this now that he is equipped with the pressure breathing apparatus, which we have obtained from the RAE.

'I am hoping to send you, within a few days, a further note on the implications of our work to date on the B3/45 and B35/46. We have reached what may be important conclusions on the undesirability of excessive sweepback, which we think has a similar effect to high wing loading in limiting the available speed range at altitude.'

Finally, in October 1948, a full report was submitted on the Meteor work, and this was acknowledged in a letter from the Director, RAE, W.G.A. Perring, on 18 October:

'Dear Petter
'Very many thanks for your letter of 14 October, enclosing three copies of your report on your flight work at high altitude. This is a most valuable piece of work, especially in view of the projects now under development.'

Among the 'projects now under development' referred to was a specification for a supersonic research aircraft with fighter factors and control capabilities, and with twin cannon armament. This was issued as F23/49 and a contract was placed on English Electric for two flying prototypes with a performance requirement for Mach 1.2 at 30,000ft, and one structural-test airframe. English Electric's proposed low tailplane configuration relative to a 60° swept 'shoulder' wing was strongly challenged by RAE Farnborough, but Warton remained undeterred.

British supersonic flight was on its way.

Chapter 8

Canberra testing...and demonstration flying

From its first flight which took place on the inauspicious-sounding date of Friday, 13 May 1949, the flight trials of the prototype English Electric B3/45, *VN799*, were highly successful. After a short lay-up from 1 June to 5 July for modifications to the elevator horns and mass-balances and to the rudder horn balance area, progress continued rapidly. In 36 flights between 6 July and 31 August, handling clearance was achieved over the whole initial design flight envelope; 'eight cycle' flutter* had been alleviated by the elevator modifications, and some 'snaking' traced to wake turbulence behind the canopy had been cured by a simple fairing.

During these tests 40,000ft was exceeded (by 2,000ft) for the first time on 11 August, and Mach 0.8 was reached on 12 August. On 31 August the initial design speed of 470kt IAS was

* Instability of the tail structure vibrating at its natural frequency of eight cycles per second.

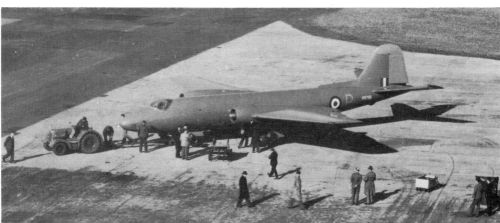

Top left *Canberra prototype roll-out, 1949. Note original 'high' rudder tip.*

Bottom left *Preparation of the prototype, VN799, for the first flight. Warton, May 1949.*

Right VN799 *airborne!*

Above *First air-photo session with the Canberra, summer 1949. The rudder has been modified following flight 1.*

Right *Superb controllability allows the Canberra to be brought close in to the Lancaster tail turret and the photographer.*

Left *Canberra senior staff at Warton, summer 1949. From left to right, Crowe, Ellis, Harrison, Ellison, Petter, author, Smith, Page and Howatt.*

Below VN799 *is towed out prior to its first Farnborough display, with the AW Apollo in the background, September 1949.*

achieved at 4,500ft, giving the required margin of 20kt over the proposed initial Service limit of 450kt IAS. In all of this flying *VN799*'s handling was smooth, responsive and stable, and with its low wing loading and good reserve of power the manoeuvrability available at all altitudes was, for that time, astounding. It was now clear that *VN799* would be allowed to go to the Farnborough Show, but it was not until the last week in August that the author could devote flying time to working up a demonstration routine — although there had been considerable discussion about it during which it became clear that, while no-one was going to say that a bomber aircraft should be aerobatted, there was no design reason not to take advantage of its fast roll rate and high-g manoeuvrability in conjunction with the lowest practical fuel loading and the best possible power-to-weight ratio.

So, on 22 August on the way back to Warton from some high Mach handling at 40,000ft, I investigated full rolls, rolls off loops and full loops for the first time; they were smooth and straightforward though they needed some muscle power where speeds above 350kt IAS were necessary. During the next week in a further ten test flights I practised a six-minute demonstration routine and then flew *'799* to Farnborough on 4 September, resplendent in renewed and highly polished overall blue finish.

By this time the word had got around and at Warton there had been some voices protesting that the prototype should not be 'risked' in this way and that aerobatics were not suitable for 'bombers'. However, Chief engineer Teddy Petter remained aloof from these attitudes and expressed the view that the flying department would know best how to present the new aircraft. This provided the necessary atmosphere of confidence, and with the enthusiastic support of Dai Ellis (Chief of Flight Test) and of flight test engineer Dave Walker who was to fly in the demonstrations as test observer, the author flew *VN799* to Farnborough on the Sunday without revealing the details of the demonstration intentions. With the aircraft fully serviceable on arrival, all was ready for the opening day, Monday, 6 September.

With the initial Avon RA1 engines giving only 6,000lb thrust each, substantially less than the projected production RA3s, it was not considered cheating to fly with a low fuel load of 3,000lb distributed in the main fuselage tanks. This led to an unexpected complication. At this early stage, engineers testing the installed fuel system had not completed 'free surface area' checks of how far the tanks could be emptied before fuel pressure was lost; for the time being this was covered by a briefed 'minimum usable' fuel level for each tank. Accordingly the author taxied *'799* out for the first demonstration using the last of the fuel in the rear tank to ensure that the routine could be flown within the centre of gravity limits by using only the two forward tanks with ample fuel in them.

With all eyes on it the sleek blue jet turned to line up for take-off in front of the control tower — and the port engine stopped. I was already in the process of selecting the forward tanks and hoped that this would restore power, but it did not and the unburnt fuel from the 'good' tanks now flowing through the engine to the hot tail pipe caused an enormous cloud of grey smoke. Now there was a dilemma, because although both the crew fully understood what had happened there was no immediate means of restarting the external battery-starting engine. The situation was explained to the Tower and a later 'slot' requested. This was confirmed and the next aircraft was called forward for take-off; but while all this was going on Petter, appalled at this apparently dramatic technical incident, leapt over the crowd barrier and ran across the display runway to his ailing prototype! There ensued some hard words from the authorities, and also between Petter and the engineers when the former gave orders for 'all the tanks to be filled right up'. I said that it had been my mistake not to change tanks earlier and that I was happy with the planned fuel loading; Joe Sarginson, design office engineer in charge, took the responsibility of ignoring Petter's order and not altering the fuel state. Subsequently Petter was magnanimous in writing to Sarginson saying 'You kept your head when others failed — take three days' leave'.

Meanwhile, the opening-day display of Farnborough 1949 continued in the hot sunshine with many fascinating new prototypes including the first public appearance of the world's first jet airliner — the de Havilland Comet flown by John Cunningham; then it was time for the last item.

With no problems this time, *VN799* rolled into its take-off run and leapt into the air after less than 700yd; I held it down until 200kt was reached and then entered a 45° banked climbing turn to the left. Reversing this to the right in a 90° banked dumb-bell turn through 800ft over Laffan's Plain, the blue jet bomber was brought back down the runway at 100ft at full power and then pulled up vertically when passing the Tower at 400kt into a half-loop followed by a 45° downward roll through 220° to dive with power off back to the western boundary, into a left turn-in for a 360° roll back along the runway from 100ft to 500ft. Next it was banked vertically left around the north boundary, pulling the turn tight at 4g and 250kt and continuing round immediately in front of the crowd before rolling out to the east and pulling up into a wing-over, dropping the speed to 150kt and lowering the undercarriage while turning left-handed over the crowd to come back in a low left turn to line up with the runway just short of the Tower at low speed, rocking the wings.

Throttles to full power, undercarriage up and then a dumb-bell wing-over to the west to come back for the final item — pulling up from 380kt at 100ft in front of the Tower to roll out at the top of a half-loop while lowering the undercarriage and bomb doors for a steep left-hand spiral down to land. But as the bomb doors opened with their normal roar and turbulence at about 160kt, the aircraft gave a lurch and a number of instruments flickered.

Dave Walker said 'My instrumentation has gone', and the author added 'So have my star-board engine instruments'. Then Farnborough Tower joined in: 'Canberra, you are dropping pieces!'

Continuing the spiral descent to position for a one-engine landing if necessary, throttle response established that the starboard engine was not dead although its instruments were.

The approach was continued to a smooth landing, with the Tower coming up with the information that 'You are trailing wires and things from under your fuselage'. It was apparent that something drastic had happened to the test instrumentation pack that was mounted in the bomb bay. I discreetly stopped '799 on the taxiway behind the wood on the north-west side of the airfield out of sight of the crowd, and Dave Walker opened the hatch and dived underneath. He confirmed that the instrumentation box had disappeared and all that was left was a handful of wires, but there was no other damage.

The flight instruments were made good overnight and the decision was reluctantly made to continue the demonstration week without test instrumentation, since a new pack would take time to make up.

Reactions to the first demonstration were immediate and strong. The impact on the aviation world was marked enough, but that on the display control committee even more so and the author was called before the committee on the following morning and told to 'tone down' the display. When querying what was meant no

The Canberra port engine flames-out at the start of its first public display.

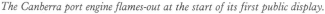

A South African Air Force Canberra — the last production series.

First colour photograph ever taken of a Lightning. The second P1B Lightning prototype (XA853) over Lancashire in 1957.

Above *Lightning F 1As of 56, 111, 19 and 92 Squadrons.*

Left *Lightning F 1A of 56 Squadron.*

Below *Lightning F 3 of 29 Squadron in a formation take-off.*

TSR2 at the moment of take-off on flight 1.

Jimmy Dell's chase Lightning and John Carrodus' chase Canberra overshoot over Boscombe Down after TSR2 touches down at the end of flight 1.

High speed tests on the TSR2.

The TSR2 after its cancellation. From left to right, Dell, Knight, author and Bowen.

Above *Close formation over Lytham — the Petrel photographed from the Sprite.*

Left *Stan Jackson's Minicab at Samlesbury.*

Above *The Italian Tornado prototype test-launching an anti-shipping missile.*

Right *The author as director of Tornado flight testing with Pietro Trevison, Aeritalia chief test pilot, and General Ciarlo (centre), CinC of the Italian Air Force.*

A Warton development Tornado carrying long-range tanks, flown by Paul Millet.

The prototype Tornado F 2 long-range fighter on test from Warton, flown by Dave Eagles.

VN799 *landing at Farnborough.*

positive answer was forthcoming, so the direct question was asked whether the display had been considered dangerous. 'Well, no', came the answer, 'but just cool it.'

It transpired that one member of the committee with heavy responsibility in aviation insurance at the Show had said that he had never seen anything like it and wasn't prepared to cover it. However the senior test pilot member, 'Mutt' Summers (Chief Test Pilot of Vickers), satisfied himself in subsequent discussion that the aircraft was in fact being flown within its proven safety margins at all times.

The remainder of the week's demonstrations were flown to the same routine and without incident, and when '799 flew back to Warton on the final Sunday it was obvious that the new aircraft had created a considerable stir in the aviation world.

Despite the gratifying euphoria after the Farnborough display it was realized at Warton that the work of getting this new aircraft into a condition in which the RAF could make good use of it had only just begun and that, while helpful to the vital establishment of confidence in the

project, the current wave of interest was based more on the newness of the concept of high jet power with low wing loading than on any magical breakthrough in design technology. The B3/45 was a good, honest, clean and amenable aircraft and, using this experience of display flying to advantage, its full potential was exploited over the next few years.

It was soon realized that within the strictly limited time available at air displays (normally six to seven minutes and often as little as five minutes from take-off to landing), the wrong thing to do was to keep on winding it up to limit-speed flypasts as was popular with the jet fighters. Far better to keep the speed down except for one high-speed run, and to spend the rest of the allotted time using the tremendous low-speed manoeuvrability by balancing induced-drag in the turns with frequent bursts of maximum power, to keep as close inside the airfield boundary and therefore as close to the spectators as possible. In the process, and as experience was gained, further refinements proved practical such as looping plane entries down to 320kt and 'inside the boundary' vertically banked turns at less than 200kt sustained with the roar of full Avon power.

The Canberra's first overseas showing was

Left *Canberra B 2 VX165 demonstrates low over the Brabazon long-range airliner prototype at Farnborough in 1950.*

Below *Canberra T 4 prototype being demonstrated at Farnborough in 1951. Note hard aileron, rudder and elevator deflections straight into a climbing turn from take-off.*

Right *The B(I) Mk 8 prototype begins its Farnborough debut in September 1954.*

with the fourth prototype, *VN850*, which was received with acclaim at the Paris Show at the newly-opened Orly airport on 11 and 12 June 1950. It had the same reception at the Belgian Show at Antwerp on 24 and 25 July, and for the next four years the breaking off from intensive test programmes to provide aircraft for Press, Service mission and customer demonstrations became a significant though often irksome factor in the Warton programme.

These frequent commitments brought valuable opportunity for practice and further refinement of what became widely known as 'Canberra style' demonstrations; and when eventually in September 1954 the first prototype of the final bomber variant, B(I) Mk 8 serial *VX185* (converted from the Mk 5 prototype for evaluation of the Mk 8 configuration), was shown at the Farnborough Show, the aviation Press described it as 'the superb Canberra B8 giving what was probably one of the finest-ever displays of a military aircraft'.

Another factor contributing to pilot confidence, and very characteristic of the Canberra, was its solid stability and aerodynamic damping which permitted the controls to be relaxed or even released for short periods if needed — for example while changing radio frequencies, cross-checking engine instruments, selecting fuel tanks or simply peering through murky weather for the next line-up point. This lack of tendency to deviate from its flight path if not continuously and closely controlled, pre-empted the 'attitude-hold' mode of later generation military aircraft autopilots which were introduced specifically to provide this facility for aircraft which were not so docile. But in the Canberra it was inherent and the pilot could relax the controls, if needed, at almost any point in a demonstration and know that when resuming them the aeroplane's attitude would not have deviated at all.

The qualities which resulted in this level of fame were not that the Canberra was exceptionally aerobatic. It was docile and completely viceless so it could be flown safely to its limits of performance and manoeuvrability at a very low speed by comparison with the minimum manoeuvring speeds of all other contemporary jets. Thus, if the pilot was prepared to fly slow demonstrations and had well-developed biceps — for this was still a bomber aircraft and no delicate fighter — then the Canberra could get more into the standard five minutes than most other jets, and could often continue to do so in atrocious weather when other aircraft were limited to radar fly-bys or were even grounded.

An important factor in this was the excellent rain-dispersal qualities of the one-piece 'blown' semispherical pilot's canopy which caused even heavy rain to streak away in lines, and which still permitted reasonable forward vision in conditions where the flat armour glass windscreens of the jet fighters became virtually opaque.

It was this uncomplicated ease of operation coupled with simplicity of maintenance and unusual flexibility of rôles, which led to worldwide employment of the Canberra for the next thirty years. Throughout all of that time a Canberra display was, for the pilot, generally a sweaty operation — but it was always fun*.

Bob Hotz, Editor of the leading American aviation journal *Aviation Week*, summed up in *Salute to the Canberra* in 1972:

'Biggest military surprise of the 1949 SBAC show was the English Electric Co's sky-blue Canberra jet bomber. . .the 15,000lb thrust from the two axial Avons made the Canberra behave in spectacular fashion. . .[the pilot] whipped the bomber designed to carry a 10,000lb bomb load around on the deck like a fighter, flying it through a series of slow rolls, high speed turns and remarkable rates of climb. . .this was the first of countless demonstrations that sold the Canberra to 15 other air forces including the USAF and racked up $240 million in sales with the cash register still ringing.

'Petter's concept of a very low wing loading, very strong structure (it could take 5g) and simplicity of systems for easy maintenance and high utilisation under field conditions has stood the test of time and new technology.

'The Canberra was revolutionary for its day (it doubled the speed of bomber forces), yet it has remained contemporary with the addition of new technology in powerplants and avionics.

*See Appendix 1.

Above *The Canberra at Martin airport.*

Left *International occasion. Martin Co Chairman Chet Pearson addresses employees before the Canberra demonstration at Baltimore, Middle River, Maryland, in March 1952.*

Below *British export 1950s style.*

The author flies a Canberra T 4 brought to Warton by Wing Commander Harcourt of 231 OCU to commemorate the Canberra's first 25 years.

'Performance of the Canberra in all its variants over more than two decades has assured it a well-carved niche in the galaxy of great combat aircraft. The Canberra success is also another fine example of what a relatively small but highly competent team of design engineers and engineering test pilots can accomplish with a minimum of interference.'

★   ★   ★

The Canberra was developed in nine major variants over the ten years 1949–59, and this involved continuous intensive test flying; but it was not the only Warton programme because, in parallel and as an entirely separate activity, the P1 supersonic research programme reached flight testing in 1954 and gained rapid and successful momentum. From 1955 onwards the Warton base of the English Electric Company was thus heavily preoccupied in extending the capabilities of and meeting world-wide demand for their highly successful 600mph jet bomber while, at the same time, carrying out practical research into sustained supersonic flight leading to a complex programme of trials for clearing its new jet fighter with an ultimate performance potential

of over 1,200mph, into service with the RAF by 1960!

It was an inspiring target and thought by many to be an impossible task.

The P1 research prototype was flown by the writer on its first flight on 4 August 1954, and supersonic speed was reached on the third flight three days later. Then, after two years of intensive research testing with two P1s, the P1B fighter prototype was flown for the first time (also by the writer) in May 1957, reaching Mach 1.2 during the flight.

The testing of this aircraft reached twice the speed of sound in November 1958, being the first British aircraft to achieve Mach 2 and the third fighter aircraft in the world to do so after the Lockheed XF-104 in America and the Dassault Mirage in France (just three weeks earlier). The test histories of the Canberra and the P1 Lightning have been covered in detail elsewhere*, but the first British aircraft flight to Mach 2 is described in the following chapter.

---

* *English Electric Canberra* and *English Electric P1 Lightning*, both by Roland Beamont (Ian Allan, 1984 and 1985).

Chapter 9

Lightning prototype high speed tests

From the earliest days in the P1 development programme in the 1950s, the design team at English Electric's Warton base had been fully aware of the aircraft's potential speed. The team knew that the 60° wing sweep of the basic P1 configuration could lead to performance far in excess of the Mach 1.2 design speed of the prototype when inevitably more thrust became available. So all aspects of the design including the shoulder wing, low tailplane aerodynamics and the irreversible power controls on three axes — the first in this configuration to fly in the United Kingdom — were developed with performance stretch very much in mind.

In the event, when the P1 prototype *WG760* began its flight test programme in August 1954 it was found to have excellent qualities of stability and control from low speed through to supersonic, but there was one major area of doubt. There was much theoretical knowledge of supersonic aerodynamics at that time but little practical experience, and some disturbing reports were coming in suggesting that, in particular, the effects of supersonic speed on airflow in relation to directional and lateral stability were not fully understood. There was some feeling that the fin area of the P1, while adequate for its initial flight envelope, might need developing for higher performance.

The P1B fighter development with a design service performance of Mach 1.7 was already on the way with the same P1 fin and rudder area, but in 1956 the P1, *WG760*, was fitted with a rudimentary reheat system to boost the thrust of the AS Sapphire engines to 12,000lb each. This was obtained with a fixed reheat nozzle which could not be reduced to match the dry thrust range and which therefore limited the power available without reheat to less than half of normal dry rating.

All this reduced the flexibility of the P1 to very short 'narrow profile' flights, but it made possible

The English Electric P1 prototype rolled-out for flight trials at Boscombe Down in 1954.

Above *Preparing for engine runs at Boscombe Down. Note ground-running intake guard on nose.*

Below *The P1's first flight. Boscombe Down, 4 August 1954.*

Bottom *The P1 on its first photographic sortie showing the highly swept (60°) wing and smooth, uncluttered lines.*

investigation of directional stability in progressive stages up to Mach 1.52. At that point the damping of the short-period oscillation was becoming slow and erratic and indicated that in combat-style manoeuvres it could become zero, or even negative at higher speeds still. Steps were therefore taken to increase the fin size for the P1B Lightnings. Thus a series of stages of fin area increase began, firstly for the basic aircraft and subsequently for the side-by-side trainer versions, and also for each increase in size of missiles and external stores.

The prototype P1B, *XA847*, powered by two Rolls-Royce RA24 engines giving 15,000lb SLST (sea level static thrust) each, began flight testing in May 1957 and it immediately showed its potential by reaching Mach 1.2 in dry thrust on its first flight. Within six weeks it reached its

design service limit of Mach 1.7; at this speed there was a great deal of performance still to come and power needed to be reduced sharply to stay within the test limits.

Within a year the Lightning had passed all its handling, performance and stability testing up to Mach 1.7 and it had become very clear that the maximum potential should be explored. There was official reluctance to be overcome however, for the Ministry had their Mach 1.7 performance guarantees and were not anxious to support 'unnecessary risk'. Also, in some of the specialist design areas there was concern about engine intake instability at higher speeds, and of possible thermal stress effects from the high airflow temperatures of 100°C plus anticipated at Mach 2 at the tropopause.

Under pressure from Warton Flight Test

Below *Britain's first supersonic fighter. The P1B Lightning prototype XA847 at Warton prior to first flight in May 1957. Note absence of ventral tank on early trials.*

Bottom XA847 *in a tight circuit of Warton, summer 1957.*

Above *A weapons system development Lightning with Firestreak missiles on test from Warton in 1959.*

Bottom left *Britain's first Mach 2 aircraft. The P1B reached twice the speed of sound in November 1958. By this time the ventral tank had been fitted.*

Top left *P1 prototype modified with cambered leading edge wings and with extended tips in 1956, for testing leading to the later Mk 6 series development of the Lightning.*

however, an agreed trial was set up for *XA847*, still with the 'small' fin and with special instrumentation, to explore level acceleration, limited handling and intake 'buzz' conditions up to Mach 2 if achievable; but it was still not given a high priority in the programme. Progressive 'opportunity' flights in November 1958 demonstrated satisfactory conditions up to Mach 1.92, and on the 25th with a high tropopause and low temperature of −70°C forecast for 40,000ft, the decision was made to go for the final point.

Prior-to-take-off checks were carried out while taxying in order to conserve fuel for this high power flight, and the Lightning was at 30,000ft approximately 2½ minutes after brakes off and heading for the first turning point at 40,000ft over Colwyn Bay.

Reheats were lit in the turn just north of the coast as *XA847* went supersonic and began its run up the Irish Sea (as required by the regulations for supersonic flight to protect the public from overland sonic booms). Levelling off at 42,000ft, speed was Mach 1.3 and rising rapidly and engine and fuel checks confirmed, when passing Mach 1.5, that all was in order. ATC clearance was given for the high speed run, and a radar fix

Above *First flight of the Lightning T 4 trainer. The author rejoins the photographic Meteor on 5 May 1959.*

Top right *The final fin configuration tested on an experimental Lightning in 1961.*

Left *Lightning flight development. The P1B prototype with experimental dorsal fin, ventral tank and ventral fin modifications in 1960.*

was taken to check actual against estimated position and confirm safe margins against booming the coastlines of Lancashire and the Isle of Man, and to show any upper air wind effects.

Instrumentation and vibrograph recorders were set at Mach 1.7 to record temperatures and pressures inside and outside the airframe and any 'buzz' vibrations in the intake, and then Mach 1.9 and into the unknown region where intake instability and high temperature problems had been predicted. There was also the possibility that directional and lateral stability might show deteriorations which could be a problem.

Mach 1.95 was stabilized briefly by gentle reheat throttle reduction and then maximum throttle acceleration was resumed in smooth, precise control conditions with no problems.

In under four minutes from the Welsh coast Douglas, Isle of Man, was fast disappearing under the port wing with the Machmeter at 2.00, and it was time to stabilize this speed for the final tests. Positive throttle reduction was needed to stop the acceleration, demonstrating that even more performance was available. Engine and systems instruments showed normal values, and the cabin air-conditioning was functioning comfortably even though the outside air temperature gauge was reading 112°C at this speed.

With only seconds left before the planned reheat-cut point, and with the Dumfriesshire coastline approaching at impressive speed, control and stability checks were made with excellent results. Then *XA847* was rolled into a starboard turn still at Mach 2 (1,250mph true approximately) for the next vital test — the 'buzz' boundary assessment.

The turn was pulled to $2\frac{1}{2}$g and the throttles slowly reduced until at Mach 1.95 reheats were cancelled. $2\frac{1}{2}$g was held through the sudden sharp deceleration until passing Mach 1.8 where the throttles were slammed to idling. All this was achieved with only an increase in intake harshness in the region of Mach 1.9, and no severe 'buzz' conditions. Then, as a leisurely descent was begun for the return to Warton, Windermere was already below and *XA847* had flown from North Wales to a few miles from the Scottish coast and back to the south-east corner of the Lake District in under eight minutes.

The ultimate Lightning series. First flight of the Mk 3A/Mk 6 prototype from Filton in 1964.

It was an impressive experience and a complete technical success which confirmed the potential of the Lightning for Mach 2 operational clearance. But there were still a number of problem areas to be met and resolved in the years ahead before the Lightning finally received a Mach 2 Service clearance. Losses of the prototype T4 and T5 trainers due to directional instability in roll at high Mach numbers resulting in structural failure, led to major developments of the fin in area and strength.

XA847 was much involved in these programmes and it was ultimately flown with low-speed mock-up developments of the ventral fuel tank and fin, and also of the main fin with a dorsal fillet to establish the final configuration for the ultimate Lightning Mk 6.

Before this, an unexpected hitch occurred in the sales campaign to obtain export orders. Potential customers in the early 1960s began to show strong resistance on the basis, apparently, that they believed the Lightning was 'only a Mach 1.5' aeroplane, and it did not take long to trace their source. Soon after the formation of the first Lightning Mk 1 squadron in 1960 at Coltishall, an exchange visit had been arranged for some French fighter pilots to fly the Lightning as a quid pro quo for RAF pilots flying the then-new Mirage. The Lightning, being newly introduced, was subject to an RAF 'initial training limitation' of Mach 1.5, and this was, of course, the speed briefed to the French pilots. However, when they returned to France these pilots apparently reported that Mach 1.5 was the limit capability of the Lightning, and this point was used with great enthusiasm and effect in promotion of the Mach 2 capable Mirage for export sales.

Ultimately, with fully developed fin area the Mk 2A, Mk 3, Mk 5 and Mk 6 Lightnings all received Mach 2 Service clearance, and the Mk 53 and Mk 55 export versions with company-funded weapons systems developments and Mach 2 clearances were successful in achieving Middle East sales. These resulted in the British Aerospace right-through training and support programme for the Royal Saudi Arabian Air Force that has been worth more than £1,600 million to Britain in exports up to 1985. None of this would have been achieved had the Lightning been limited to Mach 1.5!

Chapter 10

The flight testing of TSR2

On Budget Day, April 1965, the Labour government cancelled TSR2 with no prior warning despite the undertaking given at the end of 1964 that no decision would be taken on the programme until the following June. This action killed off what was at that time the world's most advanced military aircraft exactly at the point in the trials programme when it had become obvious, even to the sceptics, that a major technical success had been achieved.

The final year of prototype build and systems testing, 1964, had not been plain sailing due partly to technical problems and partly to complications in administration still unresolved following the government-enforced merger in 1960 between Vickers, English Electric and Bristol forming the British Aircraft Corporation. This had placed the 'design authority' leadership of TSR2 with Vickers who, although at that time at the height of their post-war successes with large subsonic civil and military aircraft, notably the Viscount, Valiant and VC10, lacked experience of supersonic engineering and aerodynamics; experience which at English Electric the P1/Lightning programme had provided in full measure. This imbalance showed in the TSR2 programme in many ways and, although the basic design philosophy on sizing, aerodynamics and engineering as agreed between Vickers and English Electric proved sound in the event, there were areas of planning in which unsatisfactory compromises were arrived at which caused lack of mutual confidence and in some cases resulted in quite unnecessary delays. A typical example occurred over the first-flight venue — a feature which would involve massive communications and support effort between Lancashire and Surrey wherever it took place.

The first prototype, *XR219*, was in final assembly at Weybridge in late 1963, and after seemingly endless delay in decision Vickers announced that first-flight would be from Wisley to Boscombe Down where, they said, the initial flight trials would be carried out.

Runway performance calculations at Warton many months previously had shown that the basic accelerate-stop test requirements essential to meet Ministry approval-to-test could not be met under experimental conditions on the very short runway at Brooklands as originally intended by Vickers, or even on the nearby and longer but still inadequate Wisley main runway; and so at this late stage I again proposed that the prototype should be moved by road to Warton where there were complete facilities for all the testing required. This was not accepted by Weybridge and finally, after more embarrassing delay, a policy decision was circulated without discussion at operating level that the first-flight trials would take place at Boscombe Down.

This decision ensured the maximum disruption in communications and logistics by widely separating the trials from both main manufacturers' bases, with the only arguable advantage that the Boscombe main runway was longer and wider than Warton's. In the event, during the early taxy trials the tail parachute failed at high speed and the consequent run-out, which would have stopped comfortably within the Warton runway, would have had the prototype across the Portsmouth road if it had happened at Wisley!

A massive prototype re-assembly and test facility had therefore to be built up at Boscombe in addition to the existing manufacturer's flight test bases; and specialist personnel were drawn from the latter to staff it for nearly a full year until the prototype tests had reached a stage fit for flying the aircraft to Warton where the full TSR2

XS219, *the TSR2 prototype, being prepared for taxy trials at Boscombe Down on 2 September 1964.*

trials, it was eventually decided, would be conducted. That much of this was wasted effort was obvious, and it undoubtedly resulted in heavy increase in costs and in a potential increase of at least six months in the total programme time to into-Service.

XR219 was moved by road in sections to Boscombe Down in April 1964, and the work began on final preparation and systems testing accompanied by an unintentionally humorous instruction from the Weybridge project office that 'the aircrew should not take leave after May 1st due to the imminence of first-flight'. Practical considerations of trouble-shooting and administration in the complicated circumstances of separation from the main bases then took their natural course, and it was not until mid-August that the prototype was even near to clearance for taxy trials.

By this time other delaying factors had become critical. The undercarriage design had not met its programme targets and, despite intensive work at Weybridge, flight clearance for retraction had not been achieved in time for a first flight in August.

Then, and of even greater significance, it became apparent that the Bristol Olympus 320X engine which was a new development of the Olympus series specifically for the TSR2 and which had suffered a number of major failures in

the test house in recent months, would not achieve formal 'type-test' for even a revised August first-flight date. Instead it was proposed to clear two pairs of 'flight' engines to a special category clearance with only 25 hours 'life'; and even this proposal began to be questioned as engines continued to fail on test.

Although Dr Hooker (Chief Executive at Bristol Engines) probably had a very good idea of the cause of the problem by mid-summer, official explanation of repetitive failures of the low-pressure compressor shaft was not forthcoming at the increasing number of urgent joint meetings now being held to review the engine programme; and when an Olympus exploded in the Vulcan flying test bed at Filton destroying the aircraft on the ground, and another failure occurred in early August — again exploding the engine and this time partly wrecking the test house — it was obvious that the engine would now become the most serious delaying factor.

Taxy trials began on 2 September without flight clearance, and with engine power limited to below 97 per cent to keep clear of the known low-pressure shaft resonance range of 98.5–99 per cent. The planned programme was aimed at establishing confidence in steering, braking, response to pitch and rudder controls, and in the functioning of the tail parachute; and based on

The TSR2 moving under power for the first time, September 1964.

experience with the Lightning programme, provision had been made for a minimum of ten taxying tests before first flight. This proved to be an accurate estimate as ten further taxy tests were in fact required before the aircraft could be declared finally fit to fly.

On 2 September 1964 the moment of pulling the chocks away from the main bogies of *XR219* on the running-bay to the north of Boscombe's short SE-NW runway for Taxy Test No 1 was one of major interest for all concerned, especially the crew in their cockpits — the author and Don Bowen.

As the TSR2 moved forward slowly under its own power for the first time, five years of striving by many thousands of individuals and hundreds of organizations were coming to fruition — it was all starting to work! The crew, totally preoccupied with observations of progressive tests of brakes, steering, throttle control, engine, flying control and fuel systems and many other aspects, still had time to savour the occasion. Now it was up to us. We had enormous hopes for this new-era aeroplane, and now it was entirely in our hands to explore and prove its capabilities.

On the first taxy tests some unexpected defects were found. The wheel brake system was immediately shown to be inadequate to steer with by normal differential pedal operation, because

when this action was applied smoothly the aircraft just stopped and would not turn at all. The nosewheel steering system was then engaged and found usable, and so the tests were continued up to about 40kt where phase-lag oscillation of up to ±2° of nosewheel proved limiting.

Double reheat engagement was satisfactory, but difficulty was experienced with the disengagement of the throttle gate triggers, and this resulted in inadvertent stop-cocking of both engines. This in turn led to loss of electrical power which resulted in the emergence of an important design fault. In both cockpits a spray of frost and snow occurred from the personal equipment connectors (oxygen) on the Martin Baker seats and also, very uncomfortably, through the crew oxygen masks. Liquid oxygen was pouring into the cockpits at high pressure! This was stopped by disconnecting the PECs very quickly, but not before incurring a high risk of explosion and fire from the possible contact between the liquid oxygen and oil or grease sources in the cockpit area.

This major problem was investigated overnight, and on Taxy Run 2 on the following day the test crew (Beamont and Bowen) found that rather coarse ground-steering control could in fact be obtained with differential use of the brakes by repeated short stabs of the pedals, and

First drag 'chute test.

again confirmed that smooth and progressive application would not work.

Excessive cockpit temperature levels were experienced and would not respond to manual over-ride of the auto-control system, and a hydraulic leak was reported by the flight test radio van which followed all the runway tests; so the remaining schedule was cancelled.

In Taxy Run 3 on 5 September nosewheel steering was more acceptable with practice and a lighter touch on the pedals, and two reheat accelerations were made on the main runway. The first to 90kt was to check progressive wheel braking and to measure brake temperatures which reached 550/450°C at standstill and dropped to 450/440°C after one minute, thereby showing that the fan-cooling was operating correctly. After a further cooling period a second run was made to 100kt and the brake parachute was streamed satisfactorily. These tests cleared the next stage for Taxy Run 4 which took place on the same day.

With 20° flap, a reheat acceleration was made to 120kt where throttles were closed to Idle. Due to the unsatisfactorily slow throttle-box action in reheat cancellation, 140kt was reached during this run and the stick was moved progressively back to check nosewheel lift. This was a smooth and progressive operation, and then the nosewheel was immediately lowered back into contact and the brake parachute streamed.

These tests were satisfactory and the aircraft was declared serviceable.

In Taxy Run 5 on 6 September maximum wheel braking plus brake-parachute was applied from 130kt, and it was shown that the resultant level of deceleration overcame the friction damping of the throttle system and caused the throttles to move forward in 'dry' thrust when they were released by the left hand in order to operate the brake-parachute handle. This would require a long-term remedy but could be accepted for continued trials by a change of pilot drill, ie, quickly re-grabbing the throttles after pulling the parachute handle!

Taxy Run 6 on 7 September was intended to clear the nosewheel lift case for Flight 1 at 74,000lb and V_r* 125kt. The reheat acceleration was normal and the throttles were closed at 120kt. Smooth nosewheel lift was achieved, but when the parachute release was pulled at 145kt there was no immediate indication of streaming and wheel brakes were applied from 140kt.

Still with no parachute retardation the handle was pulled again without effect, and then the throttles were felt for and found to have moved forward once more. In closing them quickly the HP cocks-closed position was once again inadvertently selected with resultant loss of electrical power.

Still holding maximum brake in this rapid deceleration situation, an emergency transmission was made to Boscombe Tower before

* V_r — Velocity rotate, ie, nosewheel lift speed.

disconnecting both personal equipment connectors to prevent liquid oxygen overflow.

Under sustained maximum braking, deceleration continued smoothly with the end of the 10,000ft runway coming well into sight and the brake thermocouple gauges rose to 870/810°C as the TSR2 came to a stop. With no electrical power there was then no fan-cooling available at the brakes which were released to avoid possible welding-on.

This brake parachute failure broke the continuity of successful testing needed to establish flight clearance, but it did give assurance of the energy absorption capacity of the wheel brakes and of the integrity of the system.

Taxy Run 7 on 9 September was to repeat Run 6, but the brake parachute failed again at 145kt. This time, with the throttle-gate triggers modified the throttles were closed without total loss of engine power, and maximum wheel braking controlled the roll-out in about 2,500yd (2,700yd from the threshold of Runway 24). At this point brake temperatures were 1,150/1,000°C, and Bowen reported seeing through his periscope burning material dropping from the starboard brakes. At standstill the cooling fans had brought these down to 750/750°C when the flight test radio called with instructions to shut down engines as a tyre had deflated with a blown core-plug.

This was now a disturbing situation as, although the majority of the testing so far had been satisfactory and had already produced a massive quantity of data on systems performance, sufficient reliability was not being demonstrated for the all-important flight clearance. However, after intensive hangar work over the next ten days, in Taxy Run 8 on 20 September a good tail parachute stream was obtained at 120kt and no other defects were reported other than the by-now routine ones of slow reheat disengagement and excessive heat in both cockpits.

Taxy Run 9 on 21 September produced another good parachute stream, and a stop-watch measurement of the throttle box slow-disengagement action showed 2.2 seconds as the best achievable from Max Reheat to Idle. This time-lag would have to be halved to meet specification performance, but was acceptable for continued test flying.

Towards the end of the month when it was becoming apparent that, although the practical side of the ground testing was in most respects approaching a reasonable case for flying, the same could not be said for the formal clearance documents, a conference was called by the Controller Aircraft MOS, to take place at Boscombe Down, ostensibly 'to review progress of the trials' but in fact to decide if or not the TSR2 was yet fit to fly.

The meeting took place in the technical headquarters building on the morning of 26 September, attended by Air Marshals from Whitehall Gardens, senior civil servants from MOS at St Giles Court and technical heads of the aircraft and engine manufacturers, and it was chaired by the Controller of Aircraft, Morien Morgan. Also present between taxying tests of *XR219* was the writer representing the flight trials team.

For most of the day the meeting devoted itself to perusing the clearance documents and ensuring that all the paperwork was in order for a formal clearance for flight to be given; but it was not until late afternoon, by which time the London contingent were looking at their watches and thinking of a move to their official cars, that the engine situation was referred to.

At first this seemed to come out as a comfortable account of bench testing done, running hours achieved and 'type-testing' progress; but then in answer to the question 'What is the position on flight-cleared engines?', Dr Hooker gave a clear account of the low-pressure compressor shaft failures recently experienced and said that the now-known cause, instability of cooling airflow causing the shaft to resonate, could not be cured on the existing engines without a modification programme requiring about two months' work. But, he went on, as the official 'type-test' had not yet been achievable, the flight engines had been given an 'overhaul life' of 25 hours of which about twenty had already been used up in ground testing; and that provided 'the pilot used no more than 97 per cent power for take-off and climb, the shaft-resonance condition could be avoided'. He agreed that exceeding 97 per cent could possibly be disastrous, but added that with 97 per cent at the light first-flight weight, 'the pilot would have more than adequate power'.

At first no-one questioned this and someone said 'Well, that seems to be as far as we can go'. But Morien Morgan, who always had a keen appreciation of operating matters said, 'What does the pilot think?' Having lived with every operating aspect of the programme since its inception, the main implied question was perhaps easier for the pilot to answer than for most of the others.

The writer said that the technical problems on the airframe revealed by the trials so far had either been resolved or could be tolerated for further flying, and that the major remaining problem was indeed the engine.

The Olympus 320X had demonstrated in recent months in the test chamber that it was prone to catastrophic failure in the power range 97–100 per cent, and it was clear that these failures could not be relied upon to be 'contained' by the engine casing. In the TSR2 installation the engine tunnels passed through the main fuselage fuel tanks, so that situation did not seem to imply a conventional standard of airworthiness for flight. Moreover the engine company's suggested limitation of power by the pilot to less than 97 per cent did not take into account the status of the undercarriage which had not been cleared for

retraction — therefore, 100 per cent, not 97, would be required for the single-engine safety case.

By this time it was apparent that even the London contingent had forgotten their pressing commitments as they now perceived what seemed about to be an embarrassing impasse. But, the writer continued, in view of the non-technical considerations already bearing heavily on the programme (the Labour Party's threatened cancellation of the project if returned to power in the coming autumn election) it might be considered an acceptable risk to fly using 100 per cent power for take-off and initial climb, and less than 97 per cent thereafter if no other emergencies arose. However, if this less than conventional standard of safety was accepted for Flight 1, it should not be for Flight 2 which would have to wait for the availability of modified low-pressure shaft engines.

With a clearly relieved 'that's it then' the meeting broke up, and the writer returned to the TSR2 flight test offices in the north camp to tell them the news. It was on — we were going to fly!

From that moment onwards the first flight was seen to be more a political gesture than a logical stage in a professionally conducted technical programme. Nevertheless, the trials team was determined that whatever the extra-curricular pressures the actual testing would continue to be done professionally.

★   ★   ★

XR219 took off from Boscombe Down at 15:28 on the following day (27 September 1964) at a weight of 76,300lb of which 16,151lb was usable fuel. In its first-flight test configuration this would give barely three-quarters of an hour's flying with contingency allowance; but with the undercarriage not to be retracted and severely limited engine power (40,000lb as compared with the specification 58,000lb), and fuel allowance for starting and taxying and pre-take-off checks, a flight profile had been planned for climb to 6,500ft, one wide circuit and an approach for immediate landing if necessary or, if not necessary, an overshoot for another circuit for further stability and control tests and then the final landing.

Much has been written about the first flight which was very successful and met all planned objectives. It is sufficient here to say that although hemmed in by the initial technical restrictions in all aspects of power, drag, speed, height, g and range/endurance, within seconds of becoming airborne the precision of controllability, stable smooth flight, easy and accurate circuit manoeuvrability and vibration-less and responsive engine control, all gave an immediate and remarkable sense of well-being. This was a fine aeroplane indeed and it was flying like the Warton simulator, only better!

With two full circuits completed, closely followed by Jimmy Dell's Lightning and John Carrodus' Canberra, both with Warton

Left *The author and Don Bowen preparing for the first flight on 27 September 1964. (See title pages for take-off.)*

Below *Investigating roll response with the differential 'taileron' control for the first time.*

Above *New shape in the sky seen through John Whittaker's camera in Jimmy Dell's 'chase' Lightning.*

Top right *Turning 'Finals' for landing on flight 1.*

Right *The prototype slowing down with fully developed drag 'chute and John Carrodus' 'chase' Canberra overshooting in the background.*

photographers on board, the TSR2 was turned on to Finals as planned over Thruxton and lined up with Boscombe's approach lights at four miles to go. Holding the centre-line and the approach slope (on the VASIs*) was simplicity itself, and with still two miles to go the subsequent read-out of the voice recorder went (pilot) 'OK Don — we've got it made!'

With what appeared to be (and in later tests proved to be) perfect control harmony and responses from the all-moving differential tailplane/taileron, the prototype was coming down its first landing approach as if on rails with no pilot effort at all; and although at 185kt there seemed to be all the time in the world to recheck pitch response in a dummy 'flare' at 100ft just

* Visual Approach Slope Indicators.

short of the boundary before finally flaring smoothly over the threshold to touch down at the planned point and speed (165kt).

A gentle touch down, and then came the only drama — a shattering vibration and disturbance at the cockpit which caused momentary disorientation and loss of contact with what was going on, before normal vision returned and the aircraft was seen and felt to be rolling smoothly, nose-high, down the centre of the runway. A quick ASI check confirmed 150kt and within the tail parachute clearance — the nosewheel was lowered with gentle forward stick and the parachute handle pulled, and in a smooth, powerful deceleration the TSR2 was slowed to standstill barely using the wheel brakes.

It had been a magnificent first flight, but that touchdown vibration would need attention!

★   ★   ★

88 Fighter Test Pilot

In Flight 1 all the main tests in Flight Schedule No 1 had been completed and a massive quantity of data was obtained from the on-board recorders. The summary of the pilot's report revealed only four new items requiring attention before Flight 2. These were the cockpit temperature control; the upper UHF aerial which was unserviceable; a 2° bank error on the pilot's 'head-down display' Attitude Indicator; and of course the under-carriage vibration on landing.

It went on to say: 'In this 1st flight configuration and in the conditions tested this aircraft could be flown safely by any. . .pilot qualified on Lightning or similar aircraft'.

It was all very encouraging, but now the political gesture was out of the way the technical realities had to be faced. The basic stability and control and systems functioning had not been faulted in any major way except for the landing vibration incident, but there was now a long list of deferred items to be dealt with before Flight 2 could take place, and the most important of these was the engine.

The two 'flight' engines were returned to Bristol for their modification programme, and work was resumed at Weybridge to obtain flight clearance for undercarriage retraction; but it was to be nearly two months before an adequate number of consecutive successful cycles was obtained on the Weybridge test rig.

Meantime, in a technical summary the flight development team listed their basic minimum requirements for Flight 2:

'1. Engines to low-pressure shaft modification standard and restored to 100 per cent take-off thrust with full clearance.
'2. Undercarriage cleared for retraction.
'3. Cockpit temperature control system corrected.
'4. Replacement for leaking reheat fuel pump.
'5. Throttle box modified to further improve reheat cancellation.
'6. Review engine re-lighting drill relative to auxiliary intake door status.
'7. Clear functioning and acceptability of cockpit and external night lighting.'

To these items was added a long list of work for which the quality control departments had issued 'one flight only' concessions, and it was evident that quite a lengthy lay-up was to be expected as had been predicted and accepted at the CA

meeting in September. But when the writer announced that the test crew would take two weeks leave from mid-October, there was instant response from the resident comedian at Weybridge reminding the crew that Flight 2 'will take place towards the end of October'. Nevertheless the crew went on leave for two weeks and the next flight did not in the event occur until 31 December; but from that day onward the flying programme soon got into its stride.

When the modified engines began setting-up running at the end of November, some abnormal vibrations were experienced which for a time defied identification and cure. Eventually the engine company's tester asked for a pilot's assessment, and the writer confirmed the resonance on the starboard engine and felt that it was marginal but possibly would improve in flight. So it was agreed to try, but undercarriage clearance was still giving trouble and as it was now considered an embarrassment to fly again with undercarriage 'down', Weybridge continued at maximum pressure to achieve the required ten consecutive successful under-carriage cycles on the test rig without failure, to be followed by five on the aircraft on jacks in the 'Weights' hangar at Boscombe. This was finally achieved in the last week of December. XR219 was rolled out on to the wintry airfield on Salisbury Plain on the last day of 1964 with good visibility but a look of snow about the clouds with a base of about 2,000ft.

For this flight the official authorities had insisted on a single channel warning-lights system for the low-pressure shafts, the two red lights for which (port and starboard engines) were now mounted high on the shroud in direct view of the pilot as he looked ahead during the take-off.

Protests that such a single channel system would have a relatively high probability of failure and that a false warning, if identified as true and obeyed, could lead to shutting down the engine to avoid the potentially dangerous catastrophic 'belling frequency' resonance in a single-engine critical flight condition and thereby actually cause the situation it was supposed to avoid — all fell on deaf ears and were dismissed as 'highly unlikely'.

Nevertheless it was with mixed feelings that when the lengthy starting and pre-taxying checks were completed, the low-pressure shaft warning test circuit was checked bringing up the bright red lights. Here was a potential 'Captain's decision' situation in the making!

The schedule for Flight 2 called for undercarriage cycling with observation through the observer's periscope and from the chase aircraft, and for recording of the indicator light sequence. Then, if satisfactory, stability and control response tests at 50kt increments up to 400kt, all at below 5,000ft.

Whilst taxying out the vibration from No 1 engine in the 87–95 per cent range had again been noted but accepted, and after final engine checks reheat was selected.

On Boscombe's Runway 24 the morning was still cold and gloomy but flyable for this low altitude schedule, and so with radio confirmation to the Tower that all was in order and the controller's 'You are clear take-off and climb at your discretion', the throttles were moved on to '3rd gutter' reheat with brakes released and Flight 2 began.

As the take-off roll started the low winter sun glare directly ahead caused an unpleasant mottling effect in the windscreen as the nose was raised, and direct forward vision was lost. This highlighted the need for an incidence gauge ('angle of attack') as a take-off monitor, and unstick was delayed to approximately 200kt IAS. Immediately, heavy high-frequency vibration began which then increased in amplitude as throttles were closed out of the suspect 97–100 per cent range — but the red warning did not come on so it was assumed that this was the 'other' less critical vibration.

While considering this and reducing the suspect engine (No 1) into the 87–96 per cent range, the vibration level worsened and vision was blurred and almost lost. This being intolerable, the throttle was opened again and brought a return to clear vision once No 1 engine power was above 97 per cent.

Further checks showed this to be conclusive — at power settings between 87 and 96 per cent on No 1 engine the pilot was in eye-ball resonance! This condition did not occur with No 2 engine, but the full schedule of tests was now impractical and after burning off fuel to the landing weight using asymmetric engine settings to minimize vibration, and using the opportunity for further low speed handling assessment, the TSR2 was turned on to the approach for its second landing.

Again the low winter sun straight ahead caused severe restriction in forward vision, but the approach lights and VASIs could still be seen and controllability was again felt to be superb. After a smooth flare to another gentle touchdown, within one second a massive lateral oscillation was felt as on the first landing and was so severe as to momentarily cause disorientation. Once again this died down quickly, and with the nosewheel still well clear of the runway the drag 'chute was streamed and the roll-out stopped in about 1,500yd with moderate braking.

The flight report called for investigation into and cure of No 1 engine vibration before Flight 3; for further investigation of the undercarriage structural vibration and also of the cockpit temperature control, and concluded:

'In this configuration stability and response to controls was excellent and allowed full attention to be given to the necessary engine-condition investigation. These qualities also minimised embarrassment from the unfavourable visual conditions prevailing on the approach and landing coupled with the (currently) inadequate level of instrument lighting.'

The aircraft was ready for Flight 3 on another bleak winter's day on Salisbury Plain with the rolling hills of Wiltshire, and to the south-west Cranborne Chase, white with a light covering of snow. More was forecast, but good visibility under a 3,000ft cloud base was considered adequate for the scheduled undercarriage tests. No 1 engine vibration was noted again while taxying.

Acceleration on this cold morning was brisk and the nosewheel was lifted passing 150kt with the already enjoyable elevator, and the attitude was held until passing 180kt where unstick was initiated with a small, smooth pull force. Both low-pressure shaft warning lights flickered and then stayed on!

Here it was — within seconds if 97–100 per cent was maintained an engine could disintegrate, or then again it might just be a spurious electrical fault.

Instinctive reaction closed the port throttle to 80 per cent and the starboard to 96 per cent, which was sufficient thrust not to cause a single-engine safety crisis at the high induced drag of 190kt. The port red light stayed on and the engine did not burst nor did the other engine with its light also on, so it appeared that we had the 'highly unlikely' false warning on both engines simultaneously! 'Eye-ball resonance' was again encountered necessitating asymmetric engine settings to keep out of trouble.

There being no other indications of engine sickness, the climb was continued to take stock of the situation but the red warnings persisted and so once again the flight was cut short.

Another smooth landing resulted in a violent lateral oscillation again at touchdown, and the summary of the flight report said:

'Both engine shaft overstress warning lights indicated during the take-off run. . .a potentially dangerous situation. . .

'No 1 engine vibration levels again excessive . . .and cannot be regarded as acceptable for further flying.

'The amplitude of the (undercarriage) oscillation (measured at ± 1.8g at 5 cps at the pilot's station). . .destroys the pilot's control [of the situation]. . .for the duration of maximum amplitude. This is not acceptable. . .

'In these flights involving some distracting or emergency (technical) conditions the handling qualities have been shown to be excellent. . .the ease of approach and landing including crosswinds of 13–15kt are high by any standards, and this aircraft is one of the easiest to land of any high performance aircraft in the writer's experience.'

The No 1 engine vibration was finally traced to an out-of-tolerance reheat fuel pump and, when this was replaced, further engine runs indicated that this problem had been resolved. The single-channel shaft overstress warning light fault was identified as a loose socket, and the system was removed and not continued with on the basis that it introduced its own risk factor while the shaft failure case itself had now theoretically been eliminated by the engine modification.

However, when the aircraft was ready again on 8 January, further uncertainties had occurred in the undercarriage ground testing and so a full series of low speed handling, airbrake and flap operation tests and further undercarriage vibration investigations were scheduled.

Flight 4 took off at 77,073lb with 18,330lb fuel and it was immediately apparent that the 'eye-ball resonance' from No 1 engine had been cured. This flight produced a large amount of valuable

data, and also an alteration to the landing technique when the aircraft was flared over the runway threshold without chopping the power until the rear wheels touched. This produced a gentle 2 ft/sec touchdown and resulted in a slightly reduced, though still severe, lateral oscillation.

The report summary included:

'. . .This satisfactory sortie confirmed that the basic low speed handling qualities are excellent and do not require any further development . . .for take-off and landing.

'. . .This encouraging standard indicates that the break-through into normal flight development progress may well have been reached. . .'

After further undercarriage work and some weather delays, Flight 5 was set up for 14 January with a schedule for undercarriage operations and, if satisfactory retraction was achieved, expansion of the flight envelope from the current 270kt IAS out to 450.

At 79,573lb with 20,838lb fuel, the take-off began at 15:28 in dull, wintry conditions in which the recently improved cockpit lighting proved effective. Climbing out to 3,000ft, trimmed conditions were set up at 230kt/88/88 per cent power, and with Jimmy Dell's photographic 'chase' Lightning T 4 tucked in close to take cine records as the undercarriage was selected up.

In a series of jolts and rapid changes the nose and main wheel sequence lights flashed on and off and finally showed Port Main Red and all other lights out. Dell confirmed what Bowen could see from his aft-cockpit periscope, that the nose leg and starboard leg were fully retracted, and that the port main leg was still down but with its bogie beam rotated to vertical and not apparently in the full lock necessary to complete retraction of the leg.

After radio discussion with the Flight Test vehicle, normal 'down' selection was made at 5,500ft/230kt IAS and, after a further impressive display of sequencing lights, everything apparently stabilized with three comforting green lights. Then Bowen and Dell reported that although all three legs looked 'down', both bogie beams were unlocked, not de-rotated and in an approximately vertical position.

By this time urgent technical advice was

flowing up from the specialist engineers in the Tower to 'try a re-cycle', but having studied this possible malfunction previously among many others, the airborne element of the debate concluded that it would probably be safer to try landing on the two front main wheels in their existing position rather than risk a more complicated or even asymmetric hang-up which might result from attempts at another cycle.

Fuel was running low by now dictating a positive decision, but as the TSR2 was turned back towards Boscombe height was maintained at 5,000ft while the writer offered the back-seat operator the Martin Baker option. Don Bowen asked, 'What are you going to do Bee?' and to the writer's reply that a landing should be hopefully OK he said, 'You're not going to get rid of me that easily!' And so the TSR2's first non-scheduled operation began.

With the main wheels reversed to a position in which no-one could be quite sure if on touchdown they would rotate correctly into rear-

Above *Undercarriage sequence failure on flight 5.*

Below *Flying past Boscombe tower for visual checks of the undercarriage malfunction.*

wheel contact after the fronts, or if spin-up drag would break something and cause the bogies to reverse front to back to upside-down with further unpredictable results in the heavy weight and fast landing, it was clear that this had to be an accurate, smooth landing with minimal rate of descent or drift.

By this time considerable confidence had been achieved in the TSR2's qualities of precision in pitch, roll and yaw, but even so it was with clear perception that much might depend on getting the best out of these qualities that '219 was set smoothly on its approach at its now accustomed final turning point over Thruxton aerodrome.

Confidence built up as the runway threshold came into sight dead ahead, right in the VASI approach slope with this fine aeroplane responding with absolute precision to the pilot's touch.

Over the threshold at 50ft/170kt — ease back smoothly on the stick — a gentle rumble from the (forward) main wheels — hold the attitude precisely and let the aeroplane sink to de-rotate the bogies — a second rumble and then the prototype was rolling smoothly down the centre-line after a brief and much reduced lateral oscillation. Still nose-high, the drag 'chute was streamed with its usual powerful deceleration and

the episode was over.

The bogie beams had in fact rotated back after touching the front main wheels first, correctly into rear-wheel contact, and the subsequent instrumentation read-out showed a rate-of-descent at touchdown off the scale below ½ ft/sec! A heavier arrival might have produced a more dramatic event, and this had been another example of the remarkable stability and controllability of this aircraft in pitch.

By now, with the modified engines giving no apparent trouble and with the main aircraft systems showing good reliability, the undercarriage had become the focus of attention as the main factor delaying the programme. It was now becoming vital to retract the undercarriage and obtain high speed test experience to counter the mounting media campaign which, with unprecendented pressure and clear political inspiration, was losing no opportunity to deride the potential of the TSR2 'on account of its dreadful flight test record'. It had, they lost no opportunity in pointing out, only made five flights in five months and still couldn't get its undercarriage up!

Meantime, over the New Year the government had yielded to pressure of public opinion against their proposed cancellation of the TSR2 programme, and had stated that 'the future of TSR2 would be reviewed again in June'. So in

what appeared to be a short respite, efforts were re-doubled to advance the testing.

While waiting for the next undercarriage ground testing results, Flight 6 was set up mainly for Jimmy Dell's first conversion flight but with a large amount of further low-speed handling data with the undercarriage down to be collected. This took place on 15 January and Dell recorded in the summary of his long and enthusiastic report:

'Impressions gained during take-off, in flight and landing were extremely favourable. . .

'Tailplane power during take-off and approach was noted particularly, together with the high degree of speed control in the approach configuration. . .'

Undercarriage trials were mounted again on 22 January and '219 began Flight 7 at 70,573lb, once more in unfavourable weather with slush ice patches on the taxiways and runways and a lowering snow laden cloud base at 2,000ft.

In trimmed flight just below cloud in sleet and snow showers, the undercarriage was selected 'UP' and the port and nose legs retracted leaving the starboard leg down with the bogie beam partly rotated. Once again the undercarriage was lowered (successfully this time) and the remaining schedule of simulated single-engine performance and handling completed without problems — the writer's report highlighting again '. . .speed stability in the approach and control of the flare and touchdown are a most satisfying experience'.

Jimmy Dell flew Flight 8 on 23 January on a full schedule of low speed stability and control checks; and on Flight 9 on 27 January the writer carried out an investigation of handling and landing with flaps at 50° deflection, with excellent results. But it was not until 6 February that the next phase of undercarriage trials was ready, following an extensive modification programme which had included increasing the hydraulic rotation forces at the main bogies.

Again with an icing cloud base at 1,200–1,800ft conditions were not favourable, but the undercarriage was selected 'UP' at 1,200ft/200kt IAS. This time it went cleanly away with little jolting, correct light sequencing and then no lights at all — we had a clean aircraft!

The chase aircraft confirmed all doors closed, and then 'DOWN' selection was achieved satisfactorily. After a satisfactory re-selection 'UP', flaps were selected to zero at 240kt IAS and the auxiliary intake doors closed. Now the TSR2 was in business!

With speed increasing without power adjustment the moderate airframe buffet, which had reduced as the flaps retracted, disappeared beyond 270kt IAS. Control reponses were checked and Dutch rolls* recorded first at 300kt IAS, and then with power increase and engine checks at 50kt increments up to the current flutter limit of 500kt IAS — all in smooth, precise, vibrationless conditions with superb controllability.

This run to the south-west over snow-covered Dorset was made in and out of cloud at 1,500ft and in snow flurries that made the chase aircraft's task more difficult; then, still at 500kt, a 2g turn was pulled accurately through 180° back on to the heading for base.

This was a remarkably precise aeroplane, and as Boscombe came into sight the TSR2 was eased down to 500ft, then 200ft and finally for a few miles at 100ft over the Plain and across Boscombe Down at 450kt IAS in rock-steady, smooth and precise control while the chase Lightning was complaining of turbulence!

This was followed by a landing at 160kt and

* Rudder-induced yaw/roll oscillations. A method of measuring directional and lateral stability.

moderately heavy braking to a standstill in about 800yd. The report summary ended:

'General flight conditions at 500kt IAS in low cloud/moderate turbulence at low level were extremely satisfactory. . .particularly at very low altitude where well-matched damping and responsiveness. . .added up to just the degree of precision essential for low level combat.'

This was the real break-through and thirteen more successful flights were achieved in the next five weeks.

Rapid progress was now made in exploring and extending the handling and performance flight envelope, and no further serious technical delays were encountered although on Flight 12, a first conversion flight for Don Knight, a heavy landing occurred which fractured the port forestay jack of the undercarriage although the rate of descent had been within design limits. The jack was soon replaced and on 16 February, Flight 13, Dell made the first climb to altitude and established the airframe and engine handling conditions at 30,000ft/Mach 0.9 necessary for the forthcoming flight to Warton.

The next flight achieved a double milestone in the programme — the first cross-country flight (to Warton) and the first time supersonic. Flight 14 crewed by the writer and Peter Moneypenny, Warton's chief navigator, took off from Boscombe Down for the last time at 13:13 on 22 February 1965 accompanied by Dell in the chase Lightning.

The plan was to climb to 28,000ft for a Mach 0.9 cruise to Wallasey, and from there if all was well to accelerate through Mach 1 at 30,000ft, measure stability and control responses transonic over the Irish Sea (keeping the sonic boom away from land) and then complete a radar weather penetration descent to Warton, there being total cloud cover reported from 1,500–7,000ft over the whole route. The forecast included a high icing level in the cloud and this had to be considered in relation to the lack of operational engine anti-icing systems in the prototype.

The flight went off without a hitch — stable, smooth and effortless on the climb and cruise with the Lightning manoeuvring gently off the port wing to give John Whittaker good angles for photography. It did not seem possible that this was an exotic, relatively untried and politically scorned product of the best of British industry

with the future of the Royal Air Force depending on it — it just seemed to the writer to be an exceedingly good aeroplane in its natural environment.

But there was work to do and as Wallasey TACAN navigation beacon confirmed crossing the North Wales coastline, power was increased to 'max dry' and final systems checks made prior to the lighting of reheat on one engine (for the first time at altitude). Before this could happen however, the Machmeter which had increased to 0.99 without airframe buffet or vibration, suddenly swung forward to 1.01 — the TSR2 was supersonic!

The lighting of No 1 reheat as planned was successful, and just with this power speed increased rapidly with the Lightning T4 trailing slightly until at Mach 1.12 responses and Dutch rolls were recorded, and then the reheat was cancelled. While still supersonic a 2g turn was pulled to port and transition back to subsonic seen on the Machmeter, but felt only as a slight tremor through the airframe.

With now no more than adequate fuel remaining for the recovery phase, the descent was begun towards Warton on TACAN bearings with Warton radar taking over and, after an effortless cloud penetration from 10,000 to 1,200ft, '219 was brought in over Warton for a low run past the thousands of company personnel gathered on the airfield for the occasion.

It had been another major success, and the

Above *'Cleaned up' and straight into high speed testing on flight 10.*

Below *Landing at Warton after TSR2's first supersonic tests and delivery from Boscombe Down, on 22 February 1965.*

Left *Warton sees the TSR2 for the first time.*

momentum of the test programme had reached a new 'high' which was sustained until the end.

In all these landings undercarriage oscillation incidents had continued to occur with varying severity, and now attention was focused on finding the cure. Component changes, reduction in friction levels, increased hydraulic pressure and reduction in main oleo pressure had finally resolved the sequencing problems; but now it was decided to fit a fixed 'tie' strut between the main leg and the rear of the bogie beam to increase the damping drastically.

While this work was prepared further detailed measurements were made in landing tests on Flights 15 to 20, and included landings on a foam path spread by the Fire Brigade at Warton, to assess the effect of reduced spin-up drag. During this phase the flight test achievement rate

accelerated, and in Flight 16 on 26 February the writer carried out low-level high-speed cruise tests down to 200ft in the Pennines. These were followed by partial rolls at 5,000ft and finally full 360° rolls for the first time, much to the surprise of the chase pilot (Dell) because it had not been in the test schedule!

On 7 March, Flight 17, Dell flew a flight envelope expansion sortie including handling out to 600kt IAS; but Flight 18 later the same day was aborted due to fuel balancing problems subsequently found to be the result of a massive fuel leak from a 'fueldraulic' pipe. There was a recurrence of this problem on Flight 19 on 11 March and again on Flight 20 on the 12th, but both sorties produced valuable low altitude performance data.

The aircraft was then layed up for lifed-item

changes, modifications to the 'fueldraulic' system, and for installation of the undercarriage 'tie' struts; and with these fitted for Flights 21 and 22 on 26 March, Dell flew a large number of touch-and-go landings which showed that the severe landing oscillation had been eliminated. With the undercarriage fixed down in this test case, useful simulated single-engine performance work was also continued.

Don Knight flew a familiarization flight on 27 March (Flight 23), and then Dell flew a roll/yaw gearing optimization sortie on 31 March (Flight 24).

The landing tests having been completely successful, a lay-up was begun to fit fully operational retractable 'tie' struts; but then on 6 April the cancellation of the programme was announced by the Chancellor of the Exchequer in the Budget speech. There had been no prior warning.

In the final testing period many 'first phase' departmental specialist reports had been compiled, and one main summary report was distributed to the Ministries and other authorities. These all recorded the rapid success rate achieved in testing once the major engine and undercarriage sequencing difficulties had been overcome. From some of these reports the following extracts show the general trend of increasing technical confidence among the traditionally cautious and conservative engineering departments involved.

'Flight 1. Flight Report — Summary, 27.9.64

'. . .In this 1st flight configuration. . .this aircraft could be flown safely by any. . .pilot qualified on Lightning or similar aircraft. . .'

'Flight Test Engineering Report AFN/TSR2/3 July 1965 — Stability and Control Measurements.

'. . .From the evidence available it is clear that the aircraft stability without auto-stabilisation is of a very high standard, especially at low level and in the circuit and approach phase.'

'Comparison of Flight with Simulator Results. Ae/S/224 June 1965.

'The handling qualities of the un-auto-stabilised TSR2 were satisfactory in all the conditions achieved until flying ceased. . .and the cancellation of the project could not have come at a worse time.'

'Landing Performance. Ae/S/218 July 1965

'. . .based on this analysis it is concluded that the proposed guarantee for landing distance would have been met.'

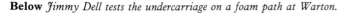

Below *Jimmy Dell tests the undercarriage on a foam path at Warton.*

'XR219 Subsonic Performance Measurements. AFN/TSR2/2 May 1965.

'The accuracy of the specific range results was high, so reliance can be placed on them. The specific range in the optimum cruise condition was found to be greater than predicted. . .'

The last Flight Operations Report (12/1) on the first sixteen flights, distributed to the Ministries of Defence and Supply in March 1965 (ie, before cancellation), stated:

'. . .the 1st flight impression of a sound and agreeable standard of stability and control in the landing configuration was correct, and. . .no development work is likely to be needed in this vitally important area, low speed stability and control being completely satisfactory over the wide range of conditions tested.

'. . .the excellent qualities of pitch control at high IAS/100ft are particularly well suited to this specified main operating zone.

'Without doubt the flying qualities of this aircraft are ideally suited to its design roles, and it is potentially a highly successful design.'

Such a remarkable level of proof of quality in the so-short flying life of only 24 flights was considered exceptional at the time by those with sufficient intelligence to recognize what they were looking at; but with the hindsight of twenty further years of experience of the costly complications, short-falls and delays in development of many subsequent military designs, the technical success of TSR2 can only be regarded as phenomenal.

The widespread smear campaign of 1964/65 implying that the TSR2 was a scandalous technical and industrial failure and a waste of taxpayers' money, can be seen for what it was as a monstrous manoeuvre for political ends from which the striking power of the Royal Air Force and the world-leader potential of British military aviation technology have never fully recovered to this day.

Chapter 11

Flying the TSR2

From its inception as GOR 339, the TSR2 tended to be regarded widely as a form of military computer with a crew of two to monitor its progress; but this misconception was in fact countered at an early stage in the design work with the applied philosophy that this of all aircraft with its critical flight regimes of contour flying at transonic speeds coupled with short-field operating capability, needed essentially to have stability and control characteristics at least up to conventional standards and significantly better than previous standards at low level/high speed. The outcome was the successful evolution of an outstandingly controllable large and fast aircraft.

A typical test flight began with the rather prolonged check list drills which have since become common to the advanced avionics generation of military aircraft, although with familiarity these drills could eventually be accomplished in about twenty minutes.

The cockpit layout, designed for maximum convenience and accessibility, was enhanced by an unusual level of comfort provided by the Martin Baker Mk 8 rocket ejection seat, and these together provided the most comfortable military cockpit experienced at that time.

While taxying the centre of gravity was controlled to the briefing value by the fuel balancing system, crew-controlled in the prototype prior to introduction of the auto-balance system.

Nosewheel steering was adequate with 'fine' and 'coarse' gearings available, but pedal forces were on the heavy side and a combination of circuit friction and mechanical lost-movement resulted in slight over-controlling which would have been corrected in the long term development programme. Even with de-rated development engines this 100,000lb aeroplane showed fighter-rate acceleration on take-off, and at V_r the nosewheel was lifted with exactly matched stick movement/pitch response with no tendency to over- or under-controlling as the rotation was continued smoothly until reaching V_{LO}*. Typically this occurred at 188kt/$12\frac{1}{2}°$ incidence, and the long stroke undercarriage action was so soft as to mask the unstick point; mild airframe buffet in the undercarriage/flaps 20° configuration giving the only physical confirmation of take-off as the wheels broke ground.

From this point on the inertia of this heavily loaded aeroplane, coupled with its low gust response wing, made itself noticeable as an almost rigid, rock-steady 'feel'. With the last vestiges of mild buffet smoothed away by retraction of the undercarriage and the reheat engine roar reduced to a quiet hum at 'max dry', the TSR2 simply did not respond in the conventional way to gusts and turbulence so that flight at Mach 0.9 in the climb, or 500 to 600kt at low level, or through Mach 1 to supersonic speed at altitude, all took place in an almost unreal calm which gave an impression of being in a fixed-base simulator and not in free flight at all!

This rather extraordinary lack of response to the outside world was matched by smooth precision in control, and in basic stability and damping (without any stability augmentation on the first prototype) which gave further emphasis to the illusion.

Even to pilots accustomed to the dramatic performance and fine controllability of the Lightning, the TSR2 was impressive at low level particularly as it scarcely responded to levels of turbulence which on more than one occasion

*V_{LO} — Velocity lift-off.

caused the Lightning chase pilot to pull up to a higher level 'to get out of the roughness'. This rock-steady behaviour made for rapid acquisition of confidence, and pilots were soon able to contour-fly manually at Mach 0.9 over hill country in completely relaxed and comfortable conditions in which even flying in-trim stick-free at very low level was quite practical for short periods.

On the climb at Mach 0.9 speed stability was excellent, and again the remarkable trim symmetry of this aircraft was apparent with very little trim adjustment being needed from take-off to 30,000 ft. The aircraft stayed on heading (at both high and low altitude at the Mach 0.9 cruise condition) without any tendency to wander off; and in the supersonic regime control characteristics were again exceptionally good as illustrated by the reports at the time. For example:

'Without auto stability in the first prototype, characteristics during 1g transition to supersonic flight at 30,000 ft:

'0.9 Vibration free. Control harmony satisfactory for continuous cruising without auto-stability. Lateral response perhaps a little too sensitive relative to the effects of inertia.

'0.94 Onset of very slight buffet vibration. No trim change.

'0.98 Cessation of any buffet vibration. No trim change. Lateral control over-sensitivity reduced.

'1.0–1.02 No vibration. No trim change. PE jump as shock wave passed the static holes*.

'1.1+ No vibration or buffet. No trim change. Lateral control response in exact harmony with pitch and yaw axes and virtually ideal for flight conditions. Three axes damping dead-beat.'

In manoeuvring flight at transonic speed the low tailplane position was highly effective in maintaining longitudinal stability, and transition back to subsonic was made even in turns without signs of the mild pitch-up characteristics normally encountered in other supersonic aircraft of the period. During preliminary handling in this area the position-error 'jump' point

---

*In transition from subsonic to supersonic flight the compression wave (like a ship's bow wave) passes back along the nose of the aeroplane and, as it goes, causes the ASI to 'jump' a few knots — and also the Machmeter, typically from 0.98 to 1.01. After going through this, the indicators remain steady all the way to Mach 2 and beyond.

(1.0–1.02 IMN*) was encountered unexpectedly at 62 per cent of design maximum thrust and this, and subsequently the first deliberate acceleration through the transonic drag rise gave immediate confirmation of the performance potential. Later tests at low level and Mach 0.9 confirmed that in this specified main operating regime, performance was right on target.

From altitude, descent and instrument recovery characteristics were straightforward and very pleasant due to the high directional and longitudinal stiffness with dead-beat damping coupled with excellent three-axis control harmony and the unusually high degree of speed stability. The confidence inspired by this aeroplane encouraged investigation of its first supersonic transition, its first cross-country flight

*IMN — Indicated Mach Number.

(Boscombe Down to Warton) and its first weather penetration and instrument descent, all on the same flight; no problems whatsoever being encountered in any of these aspects.

A visual circuit pattern was entered and flown like any other supersonic aircraft in that speed was not lost easily in level flight and high induced-drag in the turn was an effective way of quickly reducing to undercarriage placard speed (ie, undercarriage 'never exceed' speed).

The highly loaded delta wing did not permit a dramatic level of manoeuvrability in the clean configuration below 300kt where the buffet boundary was about 0.75g incremental, or in the landing configuration where turning radii greater than with, say, a Lightning and similar to an F-104 were achieved at base leg and finals.

In the landing configuration longitudinal and directional stiffness and control harmony resulted

Left *High altitude tests from Warton. The 'halo' is a reflection off the Perspex canopy of the 'chase' aircraft.*
Below *The author in the cockpit of TSR2 XS219.*

The TSR2 was an exceptionally 'clean' aerodynamic shape.

in immediate feelings of security and confidence, and a 2° approach slope was flown with unusual ease due to the unexpectedly high speed-stability which called for no throttle-juggling even when well below the minimum drag speed at around 165kt. On the approach, in fact, the TSR2 proved as easy to fly as the best of the Mach 2 fighters.

Landings in the high lift configuration at 50° flap and 'flap-blow' were very straightforward with pleasantly positive pitch control flaring to 14–15° incidence, and resulting in a gentle touch down and landing rolls of as little as 850yd without attempt to optimize either the approach speed or drag-chute and braking techniques. The directional characteristics of this aircraft remained remarkable even on the ground where

no tendency to weather-cock with tail parachute under crosswind was noted. But it was with the undercarriage that the only serious development problem was encountered in the flight trials.

TSR2 was a brilliantly successful pilot's aeroplane which, at the time of cancellation, had already demonstrated successful confirmation of its most significant aerodynamic and engineering features, and had in parallel reached a point of similar success in the developing and testing of its advanced navigation/attack and reconnaissance avionic systems. It seemed well set to achieve all the targets of its stated operational rôle, and in the process to set new standards of precise controllability which were not equalled in the subsequent developments in high performance aircraft for many years.

Chapter 12

Biplanes and light aircraft

The 1930s saw perhaps the best as well as the end of the biplane era with the Hawker Harts and Furies and Gloster Gauntlets and Gladiators in RAF service, each being possibly the best performer of its category in the world.

The author was privileged to complete flying training in this period; and to an eighteen-year-old the silver biplanes with their burnished aluminium cowlings lined up on the grass airfields in Scotland, of Drem and later Evanton, ready for the first sorties of the day in the endless visibility of a frosty Highland early morning, were a thrilling and memorable sight. Even more memorable from Evanton was the daily solo

flight to the Tain range landing ground in sole charge of one's aircraft, and conscious of the responsibilities but still able to enjoy the matchless scenery southwards from the Cromarty Firth and northwards to Ben Wyvis and the highlands of the far north: all of it with senses sharpened to razor edge by the freedom of the open cockpit, the thundering of the 500hp Kestrel engine in front, and the crystal heady air of Scotland with its salt tang from the Firth bordering the airfield giving way to the scents of heather, bracken and pines as we climbed away inland over the lower slopes of the mountains of Easter Ross.

Right *'Wings' term on Hawker Harts and Audaxes at No 13 FTS, Drem, summer 1939.*

Bottom left *The author's first-ever flight — in an Avro 504 at Chichester in 1927.*

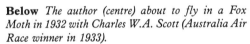

Below *The author (centre) about to fly in a Fox Moth in 1932 with Charles W.A. Scott (Australia Air Race winner in 1933).*

Above *Taking off in the Vickers Gunbus replica at Wisley.*

Below *Preparing to demonstrate the Bristol Fighter at Old Warden in 1972.*

Bottom *Flying the Bristol Fighter.*

Evanton was an armament practice camp and after all-too-brief sorties of air-to-air gunnery (with one fixed Vickers Mk II) making quarter and astern attacks on Hawker Hart-towed drogues, and air-to-ground 'front gun' on 15ft targets, we completed the course with exhilarating dive bombing on the Tain range 'bombing circle' with 'Bombs, Practice, Smoke'. Although one felt that one could have done with at least twice as many sorties, scores were apparently acceptable, and all too soon we were flying south in formation with our instructors through the mountains of Tayside back to Drem where we were to find our postings to operational squadrons.

This, too, was a memorable moment as war had just been declared, and the author's posting was to No 11 Group Fighter Pool, St Athan, to convert to Hurricanes.

Some interesting interludes followed with the monoplane fighters of World War 2, then the subsonic jets of the later 1940s, the supersonic jets of the 1950s and finally the Mach 2 fast-jets of the 1960s–70s, before becoming re-acquainted with biplanes after a gap of thirty years.

The beautifully preserved Bristol Fighter, Sopwith Pup, Avro Tutor and SE5a of the Shuttleworth collection flown in the truly authentic atmosphere of Old Warden little-changed since the 1930s, swept the years away in the rush of the slipstream past their minuscule windscreens which in fact gave much less protection than did those of the Harts and Furies! But it was also interesting to find that while the elevator control of the World War 1 types was easy and conventional in response, aileron control was almost non-existent and bank had to be assisted by rolling-moment-due-to-yaw with bootfulls of rudder. Similarly, directional static stability was marginal, especially in the case of the Pup which has to be flown all the time with the rudder; but the SE5A was a notable exception in all these respects, having excellent control all round.

This 'second childhood' experience led in 1979 to an encounter with a modern biplane design, the Baby Lakes, and it was interesting to find that while benefiting in many ways from modern practice and knowledge it still reflected the difficulties of achieving good lateral control-lability in a biplane. Owner-builder David Greenwood had made a fine job of building and

finishing his example of this well-known transatlantic light biplane design, and he achieved the 'Concours d'Elegance' award at the 1980 Popular Flying Assocation Leicester rally with it.

Baby Lakes *G-BGEI* was flown at Samlesbury airfield for PFA assessment on 26 August 1980 in calm and hazy conditions with a light wind varying between east and south-east. Of conventional wire-braced biplane construction with wood and fabric wings and welded steel tube fuselage, the Baby Lakes is powered by a Continental A65-8F engine giving 65hp.

Briefed data and limitations were recorded in the test report as follows:

Max all-up weight	850lb
Dry weight	560lb
Weight flown	560 + 80 (fuel)
	+ 185 (pilot)
	= 825lb
CG range	7in AoD (fire wall) to 15$\frac{1}{2}$in
CG as flown	14in approx AoD at landing
V$_{ne}$ (PFA provisional)	135mph (design 200mph)
Stall	50mph
C 65/max rpm	2,300
Fuel capacity	11gal
Fuel state	7gal approx (not gauged)

In external walk-round checks this very small aircraft impressed with its high standard of detail and finish, a standard which was maintained inside all visible areas of the cockpit and cowlings. Due to non-step wing roots, entry into the cockpit had to be by swinging a foot over the cockpit rim from ground level and the only safe hand-holds were the rear centre-section struts. Once this hurdle was surmounted the pilot could slide into the comfortable cockpit which is well laid out although rather cramped.

Aileron and elevator controls have commend-ably low static friction and minimal lost motion and are comfortably moved through their full range, but interference fouls were noted at the left elbow on the tailplane trimmer cables and at the right knee on the tailwheel locking lever. The rudder pedals and above them the brake pedals are easy to reach and operate, and the seat and sitting position comfortable. Fuel cock, parking

The Baby Lakes biplane at Samlesbury in 1979.

brake, the basic flight instruments and engine instruments are all conveniently placed, but it was noted that the fuel low-level indicator did not give an intelligible reading of fuel contents.

The engine started on second swing (hot) and was initially over-responsive to throttle movement owing to some linkage non-linearity. It settled to run sweetly and produced little exhaust smoke at taxying rpm. With limited vision round the nose, conventional tail-dragger nose-swinging is necessary in taxying, and with the steerable tailwheel — assisted when necessary with bursts of engine against the rudder — control on the ground is conventional and easy. Forward vision is, in fact, better than some other aircraft in this very light home-built category.

On line-up the tailwheel lock is engaged and is subsequently of value in stabilizing the take-off and particularly the landing runs in light crosswinds; but it is prone to inadvertent knock-off in flight by the right knee and needs positive reselection before landing for this reason.

Pre-take-off checks showed maximum rpm 2,300 against the brakes and magneto drop very small. The take-off run was made as briefed without early raising of the tail to safeguard against possible tip damage to the relatively large propeller, and was easy to control initially on tailwheel lock and then on rudder. Unstick occurred at about 60mph with good lateral and pitch control. A full power climb at 70mph from unstick reached 1,500ft at 2min 23sec with engine cooling satisfactory on this +20°C day at: CHT 180: OP 38: OT 95 (cylinder head temperature, oil pressure and oil temperature). Right rudder pressure was needed throughout to hold the slip-bubble central.

Levelling at 1,500ft and throttling to 1,500rpm reduced noise and head-buffet level to comfortable proportions at 75mph, and vision was comfortable in these conditions without goggles in the relatively draught-free cockpit as long as the slip-bubble was held central; but only a small amount of sideslip brought a powerful draught around the side of the windscreen.

At 90mph/1,000ft ailerons were heavy and positive but not very responsive up to and including full deflection. Response to elevator was greater and stick-force-per-g was very light. This out-of-harmony is undesirable but not unacceptable as the aeroplane remains well-damped in pitch and easily controllable.

The elevator trimmer proved very insensitive and much winding of the trim wheel was needed to obtain pitch trim zero. The trimmer 'cables' are of nylon cord and it is very likely that slip in the circuit is the cause of this problem. However, when trimmed, typically at about 90mph/ 1,000ft, the aircraft would fly hands and feet off for periods without change of attitude or direction.

At 2,000ft/1,500rpm, the 1g stall occurred at 52mph. Slight buffet occurred from 55mph, and nose drop with wing rock at the stall and a small height loss before recovery to level flight. Rudder and elevator were still effective at the stall, but ailerons were sluggish. In manoeuvre at 60mph ailerons were again sluggish and heavy, but the elevator was very light and responsive, suggesting proximity to pilot-induced oscillation in this aft CG configuration.

Wind-up turns from 70mph/1,500ft showed buffet at $1\frac{1}{2}$g/65mph, with elevator very light but remaining positive and centring on release, confirming positive longitudinal static stability at this load case. It was also becoming noticeable that in all high power-setting, high-incidence manoeuvres a smell of hot oil-fumes occurred, but this lessened with reduction of incidence (angle of attack). Engine health checks showed: CHT 150: OP 38: OT 95: 2,100rpm: 1,000ft/90mph: so the tests were continued. (Subsequently the oil fumes were found to have resulted from spilled oil when topping up.)

A speed of 135mph reached in a shallow dive to 500ft, controlling rpm to 2,300 on the throttle, produced some but not excessive buffet and noise level increase, and all controls were heavier and controllability much reduced.

Sideslips were investigated at 65mph and showed positive lateral stability either way and the nose dropping stick-free. Oil fumes again became excessive during these manoeuvres but reduced in level flight. In looping and rolling plane manoeuvres investigated at 1,500ft– 2,000ft, the heavy ailerons and very light elevator provided an out-of-harmony situation which is not suitable for precision aerobatics.

After thirty minutes' flying the absence of a calibrated fuel gauge became a noticeably unsatisfactory feature; the float-in-plastic-tube indicator in the cockpit being calibrated only when a low fuel state is reached.

On the cruise back to base for circuit work the open cockpit fresh air and view coupled with low noise level and pleasant in-trim control were most enjoyable. The approach and overshoot nose-high attitude at 65mph was noticeable but not a problem in a continuous turn Final, but the need to maintain right rudder pressure to hold the slip-bubble central which had been present throughout the sortie was becoming uncomfortable.

A left-hand turning approach was set up at 70mph from short base leg on Runway 06 with wind 090° at 5kt, rolling out to wings level and flaring comfortably over the runway threshold from 60mph. Vision of the runway was maintained over the upper wing centre-section until levelling wings and subsequently of the left side of the runway only, and the flare was easy and progressive to a smooth three-point touchdown. Pitch oversensitivity seemed close but in the absence of turbulence was not experienced.

After touchdown at 50mph the aircraft rolled out straight with the tailwheel lock re-engaged after it had been found on Finals to have been knocked to the OFF position at some stage (by the right knee). Gentle pedal braking was smooth and satisfactory.

Following satisfactory engine health checks relative to the oil fumes, a second take-off was made with unstick at 60mph into a left-hand pattern followed by a continuous-turn final approach at 65mph which gave good vision of the runway throughout. Again a smooth flare to three-point touchdown was achieved at about 55mph, and the roll-out was straight despite this time heavy, smooth braking.

In the circuit work particularly, relatively coarse and non-linear throttle action coupled with the highly responsive engine had resulted in less than desirable precision in engine control.

To summarize this interesting little biplane, it is well-engineered and finished and has conventional basic biplane characteristics but rather heavy, sluggish ailerons out of harmony with a very light elevator. Directionally it is adequately stiff but needs some rudder co-ordination in bank reversal and turn entry. The need to hold right rudder for slip-bubble central in all flight conditions except gliding was less satisfactory, and needed correction by a fixed rudder trim tab.

A calibrated fuel gauge should be fitted to

Engine running the Petrel prior to flight 1.

replace the existing transparent pipe indicator which is inadequate. (A conventional fuel gauge was fitted subsequently.)

Generally comfortable and straightforward for touring flying and circuit work, its heavy ailerons are not conducive to enjoyable aerobatics and advanced aerobatics are impractical; but as an open-cockpit experience it was very pleasant indeed, relatively draught-free and a little reminiscent of the halcyon days of the 1930s — but no substitute for a Hawker Fury!

*   *   *

Assessment of home-built aircraft for the Popular Flying Association in the period 1977–81 produced some interesting episodes. By definition the 'home-built' category covers airframes designed and built by the amateur owner without benefit of factory facilities; or else those designed professionally and then constructed by the home-builder. This activity included the home-assembly of factory-produced kit-sets and also in a few cases the end-products of apprentice training schemes, and it was with one of the latter that some interesting flight test situations occurred.

The 'Petrel' was a two-seat design development of the Proctor Kittiwake, aimed at providing simple side-by-side seater training with a tricycle undercarriage and adequate, if not exceptional, performance with a Rolls-Royce Continental 0-240-A 130bhp engine.

Selected by British Aerospace at Warton to form the basis of an apprentice exercise, the design was found to be incomplete and further

design work was carried out by Warton designers in a number of areas including aileron circuit, control column geometry, fin and tailplane stiffness and pitot-static system; and in some innovations including toe-brakes, a redesigned canopy, electric fuel booster pump and glass fibre wing tips.

Construction was mainly by apprentices at Preston under the supervision of the training manager, Sumner Miller; and when the aircraft was eventually rolled out in February 1979 it was virtually a new type.

With responsibility delegated from the Civil Aviation Authority, the Popular Flying Association monitors the design, engineering and flight testing standards of all conventional aircraft in this category up to 1,500lb all-up weight, covering the initial Permit to Fly and the ultimate Flight Certificate; and during the 1970s the author carried out the PFA tests for a number of these interesting little aeroplanes including the 'BAe' Petrel.

Engine running began on 26 February 1979 and was completed satisfactorily, but a number of items required further attention before flight including canopy locking, seat position and cushioning, parking brake lever and artificial horizon.

Taxying tests began on 9 May and these were extended to a take-off with 10° flap at 50kt IAS, a level flight for about 500yd to check aileron and rudder responses, and then conventional hold-off and landing. All these points were responsive, well-damped and satisfactory, but as the nosewheel finally touched (in 5–8kt crosswind from starboard at 50°) a sharp jolt and judder was felt from the nosewheel steering through the rudder pedals. In further tests this was found to be an unsatisfactory characteristic of the direct, ungeared connection between the nosewheel and the rudder pedals, but was accepted for further test flying.

By now a new atmosphere had become apparent around this project. What had been scarcely noticed as merely a commendable Board decision to approve a practical training scheme for the apprentice school, was suddenly seen to be a first-flight test programme on an aircraft which had been partly re-designed at Warton but which had not been subject to the standard and strictly formal and progressive company procedures of design-approval, quality control, final ground testing and Airworthiness clearance; but which nevertheless would now seem to be a 'Warton' responsibility if anything untoward occurred! So the 'Airworthiness' department under Glen Doe was deeply involved in a last-minute re-appraisal of the programme, finally giving a verbal clearance-to-fly towards the end of the month.

The first flight on 25 May proved to be a classic example of the effects of incomplete co-ordination or diffusion in the line of design responsibility — it was an aeroplane which could virtually only be flown in left-hand circles even with nearly full right stick, and left to its own devices stick-free it would roll away to port smartly on to its back!

Rather urgent rigging checks revealed a $1\frac{1}{2}°$ twist in the port wing (trailing edge up) which had somehow escaped inspection and quality checks, and this was ultimately corrected by shimming the rear spar attachment. The aircraft continued to provide interesting episodes for a while however, such as on Flight 2 when total ASI failure resulted in a handling sortie conducted without speed reference by co-ordinating pitch attitude with engine power settings in the same manner as similar arisings had been coped with successfully with Lightnings and Canberras in past years.

With the little Petrel this proved a less easy procedure due to the very small usable speed (and incidence) range; but by Flight 4 with a nearly in-trim aeroplane, good progress was possible with certificate testing, and after Flight 6 recommendations were made for a final modification standard. Extracts from the flight reports tell their own story:

'PETREL G-BACA — FLIGHT 1 — WARTON, 25 MAY 1979

One crew	
Fuel	— Full/Full
Centre of gravity	— 25.4% $\bar{c}$
Take-off Mass	— 1,517lb
Weather	— $\frac{5}{8}$ strato-cu/2,000ft
	W/V 240/8kt
	OAT +11°C
	QFE 1000mb
Runway	— 26
Flight time (1st take-off to last landing)	— 56 min.
Engine time	— 1 hr 14 min.

Stop watch zero at start up.

0 + 5 2,400rpm for cockpit contamination checks

0 + 9 Taxy OP 28 OT 48 CHT 120

'The elevator trimmer was difficult to see and not comfortable to reach, being too far aft between the seats. The parking brake lever was impossible to operate, either ON or OFF, with harness top straps tight.

'The nosewheel steering was found to feel heavier than previously and this was probably due to the new aft-adjusted seat position. It was also too direct above low speed, and this was particularly noticeable on take-off when excessive force was needed to steer resulting in over-correction up to approx 40kt, after which the pedal forces reduced suddenly to light as the nosewheel lifted at 45–50kt.

'Take-off: flaps up
  Brakes slipping at 2,100rpm
  Port tank selected (F/F)

'Excessive right pedal force was needed to track the centreline on the take-off run up to 40kt+, reducing above this.

'Smooth response in pitch to airborne at approx 55kt. Immediately the aircraft became heavily left wing low at 60kt+, requiring about half right stick for wings level at 70kt on the climb.

'This condition increased linearly with speed up to 95kt where the force to hold lateral level was considered limiting with nearly max. right stick applied and little margin of right roll control remaining. In this condition the aircraft would roll powerfully to the left, stick-free. After levelling at 1,500ft this was further investigated

The Petrel over Warton.

and it was seen that over the range 60–95kt the slip ball required a light right pedal force to centre, but that use of up to full right rudder did not provide sufficient rolling moment to reduce the left wing heaviness by more than about 25 per cent.

'With the need to fly left-handed (with right throttle) this asymmetry restricted the flight to engine checks and brief flap assessments prior to circuit work.

'Loud side tone on 130.8 and reported distorted aircraft transmission by ATC.

'Tail trim operations excessively coarse resulting in jerky overcorrections for smallest movement.

'0 + 26 Max level (2 minutes)
(with ¾ right stick aileron to trim)
2,800rpm/95kt/1,200 ft OP 47 OT 70 CHT 210

Immediate drop in CHT on reducing to 2,300 rpm.

Slow for flaps; necessitating slackening off top harness to operate flap selector lever (seat too far back) 65–70kt.

Flap 10°: lever force acceptable. Slight ND trim change. Handling good to 60kt.

Flap 30°: heavy nose-down trim change, just trimmed out with full nose-up elevator trim at 2,100rpm/65kt. Handling good.

'0 + 30 Vision forward and all round very good with high quality transparencies. No noticeable windscreen or canopy draughts or wind noise. Engine noise and vibration levels low.

'0 + 31 Fuel 85%/Full. Starboard tank selected to check transfer, and selected back to port after 2 min. because of the lateral asymmetry.

While holding wings level with approx 8–10lb right stick at 90kt it was noted that pedal-free the stbd rudder pedal led the port by about 1in (slip ball slightly left of central).

'0 + 37   Approach 1
2,300 rpm/65kt/700ft OP 48 OT 70 CHT 170
Flap 10°; R/W 26; W/V 290/6kt; Fuel 80%/F.

The left wing asymmetry tended to mask the control qualities in the approach, but pitch and yaw response were excellent and resulted in smooth flare and touchdown at 55–45kt with about ½ right stick to maintain wings level.

Undercarriage was soft and dead-beat and steering of the landing roll adequate but again with excessively heavy nosewheel steering pedal forces.

Wheel braking was adequate but not powerful.

'0 + 39 Ground checks:
External wheel brake checks.

'0 + 53   Take-off 2
R/W 26; W/V 250/8kt; OAT + 10°C.
70kt climb to 500ft OP 48 OT 72 CHT 190

'0 + 70   Landing 3
R/W 26; W/V 250/7kt; Fuel 75%/F

After landing:
'0 + 74 Shutdown checks OP 49 OT 77 CHT 165

Brakes just hold 2,400 rpm with maximum pedal force.

'Summary

'The flight duration was limited by the pilot's ability to continue to hold out-of-trim lateral forces. This severe asymmetry tended to mask what are probably satisfactory basic characteristics of stability and control, and limited the scope of the test programme.

'The nosewheel steering forces were excessively heavy and the gearing probably too coarse.

'Engine installation suitability was excellent in the conditions tested and noise and vibration levels were low. No fumes of any description were noted in the cockpit throughout.

'All flight instruments and controls functioned satisfactorily except the radio which produced unacceptable side tone in reception and heavy distortion in transmission (to Warton ATC).

'The aircraft gave an immediate impression of sound quality and good workmanship and should be straightforward and pleasant to fly.

'Better cockpit finishing would improve its appearance.

'Defects

'Defects requiring correction before next flight:

'1.   Heavy left-wing-low trim asymmetry.
'2.   Heavy nosewheel steering forces possibly exaggerated by the now too far aft seat-back (following the recent adjustment). Investigate implications of gearing change.
'3.   Radio defective.

'Additionally attention should be given to investigating a gearing change in elevator trimmer operation.

R.P. BEAMONT
25 May 1979'

'PETREL G-BACA — FLIGHT 6 — 19
SEPTEMBER 1979

'Summary at the completion of the first
phase of flight testing

'In its first six flights the aircraft has been shown to have generally pleasant flying characteristics, and the engine and fuel system have not been faulted.

'The engine installation is smooth and quiet, and the canopy/windscreen configuration does not produce significant airflow noise or draughts.

'The nosewheel steering is undergeared and rather coarse in use but this can be accepted with practice. A strong kick-back occurs through the rudder pedals from the nosewheel caster-action in crosswind conditions, and this will probably define the max. usable crosswind as 15kt component.

'Directional and lateral retrimming has not yet achieved stick-free trim in cruising flight which must remain the desired target, but the out-of-trim lateral forces are now small.

'Although negative longitudinal static stability was found unacceptable initially, this has been adequately restored (one crew) by fitting forward ballast. Further flying is required to assess the aft CG case with two crew (and the forward ballast).

'In all flights to date the aileron control has proved only marginally acceptable for continued test flying due to excessive forces and low response rates. While safe to fly under supervised conditions, this roll control is in fact inadequate for recovery in rolling pull-outs and pilots should be reminded of this prior to each flight. Remedial action is needed in order to obtain a normal "touring category" clearance for this aircraft.

'Performance is modest reflecting the weight/power relationship, but is quite adequate for the "air experience" role envisaged for this aircraft.

'Stalling, slow speed handling and particularly the approach and landing are straightforward and pleasant with the exception of poor lateral control in turbulence.

'Cockpit instrumentation has been satisfactory so far, but extensive IF assessment has not yet been undertaken.

'Recommendations

'1.   Improve lateral and directional trimming to achieve in-trim conditions with stick and rudder free at 80 KIAS.
'2.   Improve aileron power/reduce aileron force gradient.
'3.   Assess aft CG case with two crew.
'4.   Improve operation of elevator trimmer, if practical, by introduction of a trim wheel.
'5.   Pending investigation of increase in rudder area no spinning is to be undertaken; and in the event of this clearance being a future requirement, an anti-spin 'chute to be fitted.

R.P. BEAMONT
21 September 1979'

The owners and builders of the Warton Sprite, with the author before the first flight. Barry Parkinson on the left and Roy Tasker on the right.

At the same time as the Petrel programme, a similar activity was taking place at Warton with a Practavia Sprite built in a private garage by Warton field service engineers Barry Parkinson and Roy Tasker.

G-BCWH was also an all-metal side-by-side two-seater with tricycle undercarriage powered by a Continental 0-240, 130hp engine, and when it emerged on to the Warton tarmac resplendent in paintwork by a Warton spray shop expert (in his own time, of course), it looked a superb example of the home-builder's art. This was not a superficial impression and the detail of this excellent little aeroplane eventually won for it the award for best 'home-built' at the PFA rally of 1980.

The flight testing of the Sprite made rapid progress but it was not without incident. On Flight 1 on 23 February 1979, the aircraft had barely reached steady climb after take-off when the cylinder head temperature gauge showed a rapid rise. Flattening the climb to increase IAS had no immediate effect and by 700ft with 240°C and still rising it was apparent that the engine was undercooling and likely to exceed its temperature limits very shortly. A precautionary return was called on the radio and a turn downwind initiated.

However the cylinder head temperature continued to rise quickly and then the oil temperature, making an immediate re-land imperative, so this was carried out from a sharp left turn (too tight for comfort in an unknown aircraft) back on to the duty runway where, after only three minutes airborne, a smooth landing was made without difficulty just as the oil temperature reached the red line!

Handling had been satisfactory in this short flight and no other changes were called for prior to Flight 2 which took place on 2 April following modifications to the engine cooling ducting. These proved effective and in Flight 2 lasting one hour, the main handling qualities were established as very pleasant and satisfactory. Progress on the certification testing was now rapid and Flight 11 on 18 June was planned for the dual conversion of co-owner Roy Tasker.

The first take-off and circuit was flown with the pupil in the right seat for demonstration of basic handling (no wheel brakes on the right side), and positions were then changed for the pupil to take full control from the left seat.

The second take-off and climb was normal until at 300ft and 70kt the engine began to run roughly, rpm dropped from 2,500 to 2,250 and the fuel pressure began to oscillate. Taking control from the right seat the writer found that height could not be maintained as the roughness got worse and did not respond to throttle until reduced below 2,000 rpm. A precautionary landing was completed on the nearest (crosswind) runway and the aircraft stopped by the pupil's control of wheelbrakes.

Further full-throttle checks on the ground confirmed maximum rpm 2,250, with vibration and roughness leading to power surges and with fuel pressure oscillating 2–3½ psi (normal 4.5). This condition was caused by accumulated dirt and swarf in the fuel filters, and the aircraft was finally cleared to certification standard on 27 February 1980.

The Sprite was a well-made, likeable and easy-to-fly aeroplane although its performance was disappointing when compared to design estimates; the weight was up but so, it appeared, was the drag. However these tests did not complete the author's encounters with the Sprite design, for a second example home-built at Luton had been giving some difficulties in its flight testing after some modifications required by the PFA. This aircraft was prepared for final clearance by the author at Leicester East aerodrome on 5 July 1980, and it caused some surprise!

Theoretically in final acceptance form, the aeroplane on take-off with two crew (author in command and the owner-builder in the right seat) reared up at nosewheel-lift needing smart forward stick to control, and then on breaking ground showed extreme sensitivity in pitch which demanded very light-fingered control to prevent pilot-induced oscillation! Climbing gingerly

away from the busy circuit, the cause became apparent and was soon confirmed in very carefully executed wind-up turns. In level 1g flight the longitudinal characteristics were on 'neutral point', and positive and negative pitch inputs became immediately divergent — it had negative static stability! This was positively illegal, but as it was, with care, controllable the opportunity was taken to explain this interesting case to the owner by demonstration and then by letting him 'feel' the divergence!

Following a careful return to Leicester and a less than precise landing, it was found that a recent modification to the cockpit had resulted in moving the seats 3in further aft than their original position; and with two crew this resulted in a centre of gravity aft of the design aft limit! A flight ballasted to the design forward centre of gravity limit confirmed positive static stability and acceptable characteristics, and *G-BCVF* was finally awarded its certificate after further modifications to control its CG range.

Flight 1 on the Warton Sprite was recorded in the following report:

'SPRITE G-BCWH — TEST SCHEDULE
2. TAXYING AND FIRST FLIGHT
23 February 1979. Warton aerodrome.

'Walk-round checks
'Controls were checked for free movement, and no excess friction or backlash/lost motion was noted.

'The standard of finish throughout was high and there were no noticeable fuel or oil leaks.

'It was noted that the nose cowling was fractured immediately above the carburettor intake, and before acceptance it was established that this condition was safe.

'It was noticed that some wave distortions were apparent in the windscreen and these were later confirmed to be present from the cockpit. These were undesirable but not found unacceptable during this sortie.

'Cockpit checks
'Strapped in with harness tight aileron control was limited to approximately ⅔ throw each way by the thighs, and it was not possible to alleviate this by moving the seat further aft.

'As previously noted the elevator stick travel was considered unsatisfactory with the in-trim

The Sprite ready for take-off.

datum too far forward.

'The rearranged port throttle was satisfactory as was the fuel cock remounted on the port side wall.

'Some initial difficulty was experienced in achieving radio contact with the Tower and this was isolated to a faulty headset. The replacement headset produced clear 5 × 5 transmission/reception on 122.55 and 130.8.

'Start-up
'The engine started easily and quickly with one full prime of the pump, and after a short warm-up period taxying was begun in order to limit the rise in engine temperatures during ground handling.

'Taxying
'With aircraft into-wind three minutes after brakes off:

RPM — 1,500
CHT — 200°
OP   — 40psi
OT   — 35°

'Wheel braking was checked and found improved over the previous test although still not powerful, but it was considered adequate to continue with.

'Run-up checks
'With aircraft into-wind: Runway 32, wind 320/10kt.

RPM   — 1,700
Left mag   — −10
Right mag — −10

RPM — 2,350 (brakes slipping)
CHT — 230°
OP   — 36psi
OT   — 80°

'While noting the continued rise of cylinder head and oil temperatures it was decided to continue with take-off on R/W 32 into-wind in order to check if improved cooling flow became effective in flight.

'Prior to brakes-off:

CHT — 230°
OT   — 100°
OP   — 34psi
Fuel — full

'Power was increased to full throttle reaching 2,350 rpm and after slight initial steering uncertainty with the brakes, runway tracking became good. With a moderate stick force at 50kt, the aircraft responded smoothly to elevator and became airborne in a level attitude.

'Three-axis control response was immediately positive, smooth and apparently well-harmonised, and the climb was initiated at 80kt IAS in order to favour engine cooling. By 500ft however it was apparent that this was not going to happen and at 700ft (thirteen minutes after engine start) with cylinder head temperature 240° rising and oil temperature 105° rising, a precautionary landing was called for and the aircraft turned downwind at 800ft with power reducing to 1,900rpm to maintain approximately 80kt.

'Extending the downwind in these conditions showed a reduction in cylinder head temperature but a continued rise in oil temperature, and so a turn-in was set up for immediate landing aiming to touch down before exceeding oil temperature limits.

'Brief checks were made of stick, aileron and rudder jerks and the responses were good and well-damped. Control harmony felt excellent in these conditions and made the setting up of an approach to land without the planned prior investigation of slow-down and stall characteristics, quite straightforward.

'Mid-flap was selected with difficulty because of extremely heavy forces to operate the low mechanical-advantage flap lever, and this resulted in only a small nose-down trim change which was corrected by the only trim adjustment made during the flight. It was thought probable that the selection of full flap may not be possible due to the very heavy operating force required.

'Without prior assessment it was practical to set up final approach at 70kt, bleeding speed and power off to the threshold to approximately 60kt followed by an easy flare and gentle touchdown with excellent elevator characteristics.

'Engine conditions on landing:

RPM — Idle
CHT — 200°
OT — 110° rising (red line)
OP — 28psi

'The landing roll-out was true but braking when applied was not particularly effective in reducing the landing roll. It was however adequate for steering at low speed.

'After a brief check to assess engine cooling it was decided to switch off the engine when oil

temperature continued to rise past approximately 115°, although on the ground the cylinder head temperature continued to drop below 200°.

'After a ten-minute cooling period an immediate engine restart was obtained and the aircraft taxied in with the oil temperature rising again from 80° to 100° in the process.

'Other points noted

'The top rear edge of the engine cowling vibrated visibly throughout the flight and will need correction — long term.

'The parking brake operation was satisfactory.

'Throttle friction adjustment resulted in a "gritty" obstruction at about mid-throttle, and the flight was made with friction slacked off.

'In the one brief circuit the scan of instruments was generally reasonable, but in the circumstances of need for continuous observation of CHT and OT those instruments were situated inconveniently low down on the centre pedestal.

'Summary

'In the first flight aborted by inadequate engine cooling the general feel and controllability of the aircraft was found to be excellent, and no adjustments or modifications are likely to be required before continuing with the flight test programme, other than improvement of engine cooling.

R.P. BEAMONT
23 February 1979'

These were all examples of errors, often serious and sometimes dangerous, that can occur in the preparation of any aeroplane large or small, complex or simple; and they brought back memories of similar occurrences in the more complex and 'professional' programmes on military jets over many years — for example, on the second prototype Canberra, *WD813*, which ended up its landing run at Warton one day in 1950, nose-high and perched back on its tail bumper with its centre of gravity wrongly controlled by ballast and fuel scheduling to beyond the aft limit!

There were also a number of examples of ASI failure in Canberra and Lightning testing, some of which resulted from poor instrumentation design and all leading to interesting landings; and further back still, a Tempest on test which returned with tight and jamming elevator control due, it was found, to the test instrumentation

pack having been strapped on to its tray tightly round the elevator control runs!

By contrast, the first light aeroplane tested by the author for the PFA was Gardan Minicab *G-AWEP*, built by enthusiast Stan Jackson, superintendent of the plating and processing department of the great English Electric (later British Aerospace) factory at Preston. This aeroplane was a remarkable example of the quality which can be achieved by a combination of skills, knowledge, enthusiasm and dedication; and in its test programme and a decade of subsequent pleasure flying 'Echo Papa' gave no serious problems at all and a remarkable level of reliability.

Basically of wood and fabric construction and with a Rolls-Royce Continental C90 engine of 90bhp, the Minicab weighed under 1,100lb with fuel and one crew and it was a delightful if rather delicate aeroplane both to fly and maintain. In the air it was much affected by gusting winds and

general turbulence, and in the hangar it was prone to all-too-easy damage from spanners dropped through its fabric or unauthorized boots climbing over it!

Nevertheless, with sparkling performance, light control harmony, well-damped and stable flight characteristics and the ability to land with full flap into a 10kt wind in under 50yd (and sometimes across the main runway at Warton in crosswinds which would otherwise have been too strong for it), it was one of the most pleasurable aeroplanes in forty years.

Used frequently for home-to-work commuting between Samlesbury aerodrome and Warton, it began and ended the day on a high note and sometimes gave moments of unusual fascination, such as when meeting and joining formation with a skein of pinkfoot geese heading into a stormy sky over the Ribble estuary one winter's morning on the way to work over the rush-hour traffic jams.

Left *Minicab owner Stan Jackson swings the propellor for the first flight, from Samlesbury.*

Right *VIP flight for the Minicab. Lord Lieutenant of Lancashire Simon Towneley about to fly with the author at Samlesbury.*

'MINI-CAB G-AWEP — FLIGHT REPORT NO 1, SAMLESBURY 21 JUNE 1969

Fuel 11gal
1 crew
Weight 1,027lb
C.G. 15.03in
Weather: Wind 190° 15–18kt gusting 6/8ths/2,500ft. Visibility 10 miles.
Take-off: Runway 18

Engine start satisfactory on first swing after two primes.

1,200rpm, oil pressure 32psi, oil temperature 30°F, cylinder head temperature 90°C. Altimeter set 996 millibars.

'On the ground, stationary and while taxying, the fresh air provided by the new air vent on the port rear cabin window was satisfactory.

'Run-up checks

Idling: 600rpm, 95°F, 30psi, Cylinder 150°C

Full power 2,250, 110°F, 35psi, Cylinder 200°C
No 1 Mag switch off, 2,200rpm
No 2 Mag switch off, 2,250rpm

'At the end of these engine checks the cylinder head temperature was 230°C, and a fairly strong hot engine smell was present.

'While taxying at approximately 1,000rpm the cylinder head temperature dropped quite rapidly and had levelled at 155°C on reaching the runway.

'Prior to take-off checks

Idle 600rpm 150°F 18psi
Cylinder 155°C
Max power 2,250rpm Suction 4.25in.

'With max. throttle set and trimmer neutral, flaps up, the tail was lifted smoothly with gentle forward stick movement and lift-off occurred after less than 200yd at approximately 45kt.

'500ft   70kt   2,250rpm   170°F
32psi   Cylinder 210°C

'Longitudinal control light, responsive with good damping. Lateral control light, responsive with good damping. Directional damping less good with tendency for the slip ball to wander.

'Engine noise and vibration levels in max. power climb moderate and satisfactory.

'Cruise at 1,000ft/2,000 rpm.

'After two minutes ASI 81kt. Trim (elevator) at the zero notch as for take-off. Noise level low and pleasant. Cabin air fresh with port vent open.

'After three minutes cruise in these conditions, ASI 86kt, 2,000rpm, 180°C, 30psi, Cylinder 170°C, Suction 8.5in. Power reduced to 1,850rpm and speed stabilized at 79kt in slight turbulence.

'Control checks
'The pitch control was satisfactorily responsive and well damped, and lateral displacements resulted in good response coupled with a slight recovery tendency, i.e, positive rather than the more normal neutral stability. This was not an adverse feature as it contributed to maintaining wings level, hands off.

'Response to rudder input resulted in adequate control in yaw but in less satisfactory damping, and in the prevailing turbulence as well as following deliberate rudder inputs, rather low weather-cock stability was noticeable. The slip-ball was active throughout the flight and fairly continuous small amplitude rudder co-ordination was necessary to maintain slip ball zero, especially in turbulence. It was also noted that full power acceleration in take-off, climb or level flight required left rudder to counteract propeller torque. In smooth air control harmony was excellent, but in turbulence and in maneouvre the need to co-ordinate with rudder was noticeable.

'In deliberate Dutch roll oscillation the lack of weather-cock stability was noticeable, damping being "soggy" with failure of the down-going wing to recover, and side-slip remaining on initially pedal-free.

'The initial climb and subsequently whenever maximum power was used a heat source was noticed under the legs and this became quite uncomfortable when combined with solar radiation. The fresh air vent provided adequate cooling air, and was clearly very essential under these circumstances. No oil or petrol fumes were present, and the hot engine smell became less apparent as the flight progressed and was no problem.

'Slow down 1,000ft clean configuration.

'IAS was reduced to 44kt where slight wing rocking occurred accompanied by reduced control responsiveness.

'Slow down 2,100ft, 15° flap. Very slight nose down trim change.

'42kt slight buffet and slight nose drop.

'Slow down 3,100ft, full flap at 50kt. Slight nose down trim change.

'At 40kt, slight wing drop and further nose down trim with tendency to yaw to starboard.

'Recovery commenced from 39kt.

'In these tests the variation of trim with flap was no more than 1–2lb on the stick and scarcely required trimmer adjustment. Engine control at low speeds remained smooth and excellent, and there was no sign of plug roughness on opening up after 1–2 minutes at tick-over.

'Max. level 1,000ft.

'After one minute at 2,250rpm, ASI 105kt increasing, 180°F, 32psi, Cylinder 195°C.

'A very slight nose-down trim adjustment was necessary between 80 and 100kt.

'Throughout these checks the elevator trim tab control range was adequate for the very small adjustments necessary, but the slack and stretch in the cable made trim adjustments rather imprecise.

'A normal approach was made for landing 1, with power set to control the descent at 60kt initially reducing to 55kt to set take-off (15°) flap.

'The slight nose down trim change resulting required a small trimmer adjustment, and the final approach was flown at 55kt to threshold for a touchdown at approximately 42kt on the main wheels before closing power. This landing was relatively smooth and the subsequent roll out was controlled reasonably easily, though the relationship between the foot position on the rudder pedals and the heel position on the brakes was not easy to achieve smoothly, largely due to the incorrect position of the starboard brake pedal relative to the starboard rudder pedal.

'In take-off 2 the lift-off was achieved in approximately 150yd against a 15kt wind and an approach set up with 2 notches flap (30°). This required the elevator trim tab setting back 1in from neutral on the wheel.

'The approach was pleasant and satisfactory at 50kt and power was cut during flare for a three point touchdown at approximately 40kt.

'After taxying, engine checks before shut down: 2,250rpm, 190°F, 32psi, Cylinder 185°C.

'Summary

'The engine, fuel and electrical systems functioned completely satisfactorily, and the engine was smooth, responsive, remarkably quiet in the cruising range, and generally conducive to confidence.

'The flying controls with their previously noted low static friction were pleasant and responsive in flight; and positive longitudinal stability, slightly positive lateral stability, and positive but low weather-cock stability added up to pleasant control harmony and an easily flown aeroplane.

'The latter characteristics of low weather-cock stability necessitates rudder co-ordination for accurate flying and results in a less than crisp aeroplane directionally. This is an area which could be improved with advantage. Take-off presents no problems, but the landing with sensitive longitudinal control and relatively nose-high attitude coupled with vision distortion through the windscreen transparencies, is not easy to get right first time and is likely to require practice.

'With the elevator tab trim wheel set at the neutral notch very little retrimming is required in flight, but the trimmer range at "Full Nose-up" is not quite sufficient to trim out full flap in the FWD/CG case with one crew. Flight time 25 minutes.

R.P. BEAMONT'

Chapter 13

Testing an ultralight aeroplane

The Wren was an entry for an Air Ministry competition in 1923 for an ultralight training aircraft. It was built by English Electric at Preston to the design of W.O. Manning, who came back to Warton at the age of eighty in 1960 to see it fly again at the Company's test airfield which was dominated at the time by Canberra jet bombers and the P1 supersonic fighter prototypes.

The Wren was powered by a 398cc ABC engine which had been developed for a moderate-sized motor cycle, and it was entered for the *Daily Mail* Light Aeroplane competition at Lympne where it achieved a joint class win (together with the ANEC) by flying an astonishing 87.5 miles on one gallon of fuel.

Embodying the relatively new departure for that time of a cantilever monoplane wing, Manning intended that the aeroplane should attain as far as possible the efficiency of a glider; to do this he produced a very clean structure with slim fuselage and a narrow track undercarriage with wheels three-quarters submerged in the fuselage, and with the pilot virtually sealed in the deep cockpit behind the engine by a fabric apron which clipped round his neck! There was no such refinement as a windscreen, presumably on the basis that the performance would hardly necessitate one, and the designer was quite right on that score!

In 1955 a small team of wood and fabric workers from the old Vampire production organization at English Electric, headed by test pilot Peter Hillwood and development engineer Bill Eaves, had rebuilt the aircraft (which is now at the Shuttleworth Collection at Old Warden) from components of one aircraft that had been stored in the factory roof at Strand Road, Preston,

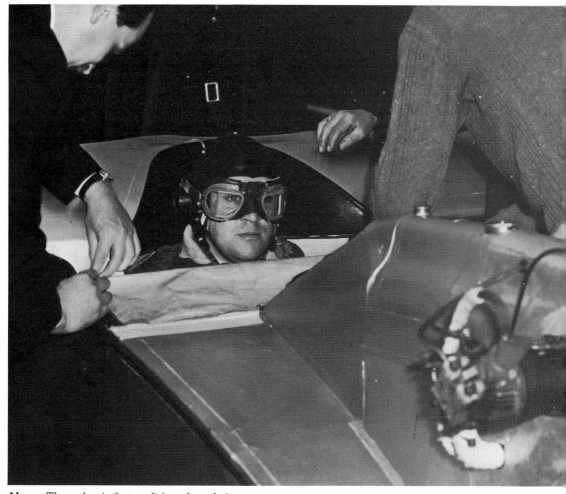

Above *The author is 'buttoned' into the cockpit.*

Left *Peter Hillwood taxies out for the first flight of the Wren after restoration, Warton, 1955.*

since it last flew as the competition winner in the 1920s. Components from the remains of a second aircraft which had been located on a farm in Dumfriesshire were also used.

The overhauling and rebuilding of vintage aeroplanes requires three main ingredients: money, skill and dedication, and in the case of the Wren the last two were available in good measure. However the budget was small and when, after stripping the engine and replacing valve guides and springs, the first engine runs suggested low compression and very little power output, the team had to make the best of it.

Hillwood, a twelve-stone six-footer, provided a formidable load for such a little aeroplane, but

after a number of taxy runs along Warton's main runway he coaxed it into the air for a straight hop. Reporting that it handled very well in pitch and yaw and adequately in roll, he said that it didn't appear to want to climb out of ground effect and that, as expected, the landing roll was difficult to keep straight due to the hard tailskid (on the asphalt runway). Taxying could only be done with 'steerers' at the wing tips of course.

Eventually Hillwood got the Wren up to 200–300ft for circuits on a number of occasions, and so it was decided to try the author's thirteen stone in it!

The pilot sits virtually on the floor of the fuselage in a small and original wicker-work seat,

Press day! The Wren flies over the P1 at Warton.

and with the 'apron' round one's neck there is no vision of the stick, throttle and mixture levers or the all-important drip-feed valve, so that control is by 'Braille'. The dominant impression gained is that one's bottom must be almost touching the ground, and that forward vision is restricted by both large ASI and rpm gauges mounted on the fuel tank at the back of the engine, and by the open ends of the two exhaust stubs at about eye level!

The engine starts readily and runs smoothly but, of course, noisily at such close proximity, and with a shove from the wing-tip handlers the Wren quickly gathers sufficient speed for adequate rudder control. Then the narrow wheel track makes itself felt by an early rolling tendency which is easily controlled with aileron, and the tail must be raised to take-off attitude with positive forward stick as there is clearly insufficient power for prop-wash to raise it unaided — and here is the first problem. With such marginal power the effect of increased drag is large and immediate; too coarse use of elevator, rudder and ailerons can so reduce acceleration as to prolong or even prevent take-off.

On this flight at a maximum take-off rpm of about 2,150 and in almost calm air, speed built up with the tail high to about 27mph and appeared to stick there until about half a mile of runway had passed, when at about 28mph the wheels stopped rumbling. Holding it level, speed built up very slowly to about 34mph and then, while easing into a gentle climb, dropped rapidly to 27 again. The aircraft then stopped climbing in the classic situation of running out of runway but with insufficient height to turn. So very gingerly the height gained was eased from 100ft back to 50ft, regaining speed to 34mph. This in fact worked and a just-positive climb was maintained at 29–30mph until back at about 150ft and now outside the airfield boundary.

Warton is on low marshland but has buildings and hedges surrounding it, and the author had never before realized what mighty obstructions to aviation these were!

It was apparent that the rpm was fading at this point and that a normal circuit was not going to be achieved; so keeping control movements to the bare minimum the Wren was eased into a turn to starboard, when it immediately started losing height as the induced-drag increased.

Deciding that a circuit was not going to be possible and that it was a case of first things first, the turn was kept going and descending until, after 180°, the Wren was heading back towards the boundary with a positively enormous tree just ahead (in fact a 20ft tamarisk bush). Diving off the remaining height directly at the bush, temporarily restored ASI to about 32mph and permitted a hop over the bush at the last moment into the clear flat plain of the airfield, and even though 'downwind' in a very light breeze there seemed at least a chance of regaining the runway.

At this point and now very low over the grass, the Wren started to fly again, clearly benefiting from ground effect; but maximum rpm had now dropped to 2,000 due to overheating and it was simple to organize the aeroplane with its surprisingly responsive controls and excellent stability to a gentle landing which only ground-looped slightly at the end due to the 5kt tail wind.

In subsequent flights with the oil-drip feed properly controlled to prevent overheating at 2,300 engine rpm, it was established that with its clean aerodynamics, long tail arm and generous control surfaces, the Wren had basic longitudinal and directional static stability and neutral lateral stability, and that these together with good pitch and yaw response and good harmony in stick forces added up to a very pleasant and conventional aeroplane; that is in all but the power/weight ratio sense!

In 1975 the engine was worked over at Old Warden by Wally Berry who succeeded in restoring it to 2,500 rpm at which, in the capable hands of Desmond Penrose, it showed take-off and circuit capability from the Old Warden grass together with a maximum level speed of 40mph, stall buffet at 24mph and no untoward characteristics in a shallow dive to 70mph. All quite remarkable for a 55-year-old design and on only 3 nominal hp.

The Wren has shown itself to be a very pleasant, straightforward aeroplane in the air, but primarily that with an engine of twice the power it could have been a very likeable little sporting aeroplane. It was a remarkable design achievement and much ahead of its time.

Chapter 14

Fw 190 replica

Two dates — 13 September 1943 and 30 March 1980 — had a certain similarity for the author as both involved flights in 'Fw 190s'. The first was the original Focke Wulf captured intact in 1943 when it landed at Fairwood Common in South Wales, and the second was a surprisingly close replica to $\frac{1}{2}$ scale built in 1979 by Mike Searle of Aero Services Ltd at Elstree. There the similarity might have ended for the wood and glass fibre construction replica weighed only 1,010lb with its 100hp Continental 0-200-A engine, while the original weighed 8,600lb and had around 1,700hp from its fan-cooled BMW 801-D radial 14-cylinder, twin row engine; but there turned out to be other interesting similarities.

The replica, *G-WULF*, designed by War Aircraft Replicas in America, had a span of 26ft and length 16ft, so it was a very small aeroplane indeed and gave a first impression on close acquaintance that it had escaped from a model aircraft rally. In general appearance it was an almost true replica of the real thing with wing, rear fuselage and tail, undercarriage and under-fuselage bomb/long-range tank rail all looking accurate. The cockpit area was realistic also with a true-looking windscreen and canopy profile; but the rear half of the canopy let the accuracy down as the transparency was cut off just behind the dummy armour-plate where, on the original, an outstanding feature was the long clear-view rear canopy extending half-way to the tail.

Forward of the windscreen the engine cowling was a clever simulation of the original with the exhaust system terminating realistically in four ejector stubs a side, three of which were dummies. Only a look through the nose intake revealed not a lusty twin-row radial engine but the 0-200-SA which was well cooled without benefit of the original's fan cooling.

The propeller was of wood, three-bladed, skinned in GRP (glass-reinforced plastic) and finished in black, and with a well-proportioned black spinner painted with the white spiral of the period it all looked very realistic. Only a long, critical look revealed two basic dissimilarities; the wing had noticeably less dihedral and the cockpit/windscreen was slightly further aft than on the original. Nevertheless, without another aircraft to give it scale the replica did look very like its exciting original and in flight the sight of it seemed likely to give cold shivers to World War 2 veterans!

Walk-round checks showed a high standard of skinning and detail finish, and commendably low static friction on all controls and absence of noticeable backlash. The tailwheel was steered through conventional springs and the retracting undercarriage was noted to have a comfortingly simple linkage and geometry. It was thought likely to be prone to the accumulation of mud/grit from the wheels (shod with go-cart tyres!), and that this would need to be the subject of regular maintenance checks.

Climbing into the cockpit of this aircraft was, for this low aspect ratio pilot, akin to pulling on rather tight trousers, and in fact getting out of it subsequently was the only difficult part of the whole operation! However, once seated in the comfortable semi-reclining seat with the feet resting on the rudder pedals virtually under the rear of the engine, it proved to be a comfortable cockpit with all controls and switches within easy reach.

Of particular interest was the stick grip which, while providing a reasonable representation of the shaped grip of the original '190, was in practice an American P-86 style stick and very comfortable in use.

The report (abbreviated) on this flight recorded the following:

'*G-WULF* Popular Flying Association assessment — Leicester East.

'The aircraft was flown (for PFA permit assessment) in moderate/improving weather conditions, and in the presence of light training and club traffic which limited some aspects of the tests.

'The cockpit, though appearing very small, proved to be comfortable when settled and strapped in. The Zlin five-point harness installed was cumbersome to fit but comfortable with good restraint when adjusted.

'All controls and switches could be reached and operated with straps tight, and full control deflections could be achieved although full aileron with "up" elevator was resisted by the thighs.

'Instrument panel layout was easily identified and well captioned, but vision of ASI and Rev counter was restricted at the top third by the coaming and the E2 compass. Grouping of engine references was haphazard with cylinder head temperature (CHT) top left, oil pressure (OP) and temperature (OT) bottom left, Amps bottom centre and rpm top right. A more suitable arrangement would be conventional grouping of all these below/right of the rpm gauge.

'The tail-down, nose-high attitude was marked when strapped in, and with the canopy shut head movement was restricted.

'Engine start immediate. Ground idle 600rpm; fuel 11gal CHT 150° OP 45 OT 55 Amps +1.

'The flying controls were free of noticeable static friction and backlash, and the throttle and fuel cock were well-positioned and easy to operate.

'The rudder pedals were found to have a noticeable amount of fore/aft spring-loaded free play when both pedals were equally depressed (not brake pedal rotation). This proved to be undesirable in taxying and take-off/landing run control, as it reduced direct feel of tailwheel steering.

'With no parking brake, starting and ground-running required restraint by brake pedal operation which proved adequate.

'View ahead was largely obscured by the high nose, and safe taxying required swinging the nose (as did the original Fw 190). Tailwheel steering was adequate once the fore/aft rudder pedal movement had been allowed for.

'With cold outside air temperature (OAT) (+6°C) the small windscreen and canopy misted

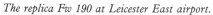

The replica Fw 190 at Leicester East airport.

Left *The author flying the 'Fw 190' from Leicester.*

Right *The '190' being flown by its owner/builder, Mike Searle.*

quickly with canopy shut, and the absence of a fresh air vent was noted.

'When checking the movements needed for activation of the manual undercarriage emergency DOWN selection it was felt that this was likely to be a difficult operation.

'At full power, acceleration was brisk but there was no tendency for self-lift of the tail which needed light but positive forward stick to achieve take-off attitude. Prior to this, total lack of forward vision resulted in some slight veering about the runway centre-line.

'Unstick at approx 55kt and initial climb held at a comfortably steep angle at 70kt. Undercarriage retraction complete in 9.5 sec. Red and Green indicator lights satisfactory. No noticeable trim change, noise or buffet associated with undercarriage down, or when retracting.

'Three-axis control responses, 1,000ft/100kt: Pitch — light, positive and dead-beat; Aileron — light, crisp and dead-beat; Rudder — very light and powerful, but well damped.

'Aileron/elevator harmony excellent, but rudder lighter and out of harmony. However, it was soon apparent that with excellent weathercock stability and crisp response and damping in all axes, rudder co-ordination was seldom necessary and its lightness was not noticeable

except when deliberately assessing sideslips etc.

'Rolling power was high with 360° barrel rolls executed smoothly at 100°/sec+, and about 2.5lb to full deflection.

'Stick force per g was light at 1.5lb/g estimated, but with no noticeable static friction or backlash and with dead-beat damping these low values were very satisfactory for fighter-type manoeuvrability. Crisp "hesitation" rolls were practicable.

'At all speeds above 100kt, rpm needed controlling against overspeeding and this was easy to manage with smooth, responsive throttle, but had to be remembered.

'IAS increased to 165kt (V_{ne} 175) in shallow dive with only moderate increase in noise level, and all control responses as before though heavying slightly. Noticeable in mild turbulence that tracking accuracy remained dead-beat and excellent.

'2,000ft: 9.5gal, slowdown to "clean" stall.

'As IAS reduced below 60kt for the first time in the flight a nose-up trim adjustment would have been needed for stick-free trim, but was not made.

'Stall 42kt. Slight buffet from 43kt. Left wing smooth roll away, checked instantly by small forward stick.

'Repeat gear down. Effects of gear lowering at

70kt hardly noticeable. Stall buffet as before 43kt; left wing drop at 42kt.

'Throttle response at stall good.

'From 70–160kt the aircraft remained in lateral and directional trim controls-free and needed hardly any pitch adjustment.

'Longitudinal static stability was positive and well damped throughout the speed range 42–160kt.

'Sideslips — 1,500ft. 1.3 V_s power on. 9gal.

'Left and right rudder. Strong weathercock stability and light aileron force to hold. (Positive lateral stability, sideslipped wing rises.)

'During all low engine-power points the undercarriage warning horn operated correctly with acceptable noise level in the headset.

'Right-hand circuit and approach to runway 28.

'At 70kt and below, the very nose-high attitude was restrictive and confirmed that straight-in approaches would be unsuitable for this aircraft below about 80kt (which would result in the complication of losing excess speed on this flapless aircraft during final approach).

'On overshoot from 100ft/70kt about ⅔ throttle gave good response and a steep climb while retracting undercarriage from 80kt — time 12sec.

'Left-hand circuit and continuous curve approach at 70kt maintained vision of the threshold until rolling out and flaring at about 10ft when all forward vision was lost, direction having to be maintained by alternate side viewing of the runway edges.

'Control in the flare was precise on all axes and it was easy to hold level as speed bled off slowly in a long float until gentle touchdown, but in the initial roll-out some veering occurred due to the restricted vision references coupled with rudder pedal "sponginess".

'After a second take-off:

'From 2,000ft/90kt. Left turn dynamic stall. 7gal.

'Power increased to achieve 3g/70kt in level turn. Left wing drop with short buffet. Stopped immediately with slight forward stick.

'Repeat in right turn with same result. If stick held at wing-drop the incipient spin would develop but was controllable with forward stick. This was not investigated beyond ½ turn.

'Wing-overs from 120–60kt and loops from 160kt were smooth and elegant, but if pulled too tight below 75kt would depart left-wing with recovery as above.

'Engine smooth and responsive with stable indications and good cooling throughout.

'No fuel or other fumes were noted throughout

this 1.10 hr flight, and radio performance on 122.25 with RAF inner helmet and 1945-standard mask/headset, clear and satisfactory.

'Final left-hand continuous curve approach at 70kt satisfactory.

'Roll-out and flare over threshold at 67kt and long "blind" float before gentle touchdown on final landing. Braking action smooth, but difficult to prevent veering until slow speed for the reasons above.

'Conclusions
'*G-WULF* has been described by Mr F.I.V. Walker* as well-built to professional standards. Flight experience supports this and the aircraft has exceptional control qualities for any aircraft in this category. It is a pleasure to fly and well within the capabilities of suitably experienced tailwheel pilots, with the one exception that forward view is not merely restricted but is non-existent for straight taxying and in straight-in approaches. This aspect will need to be covered in Pilots' Notes and by strict supervision of conversion training. It could use a wing-flap system.

'The aircraft was not found to have any other vices, although its tendency to roll out of looping plane manoeuvres into incipient spin if uncorrected needs taking account of in planning flight demonstrations.

'Full performance measurements were not made on this flight, but there is a comfortable excess of power for missed approaches without swing or trim changes. One minute stabilizations at 1,000ft showed 135kt at 2,500rpm, and 150kt at 2,750.

'Its mini-fighter style qualities are enjoyable and confidence-making to a point which might cause inexperienced pilots to exceed their own capabilities, and this must be guarded against.'

★   ★   ★

In all a very attractive high-performance single-seat aeroplane with high quality and predictable control characteristics, generally symmetrical trimming and a smooth engine installation helped undoubtedly by the three-blade propeller; but an aircraft which needed supervision in conversion training due to severely limited forward vision in its necessarily flapless approaches which tended to result in excessive threshold speeds, long floats and hold-offs and therefore relatively lengthy landing runs, particularly if associated with wet grass. This was a fun aeroplane of high quality, and a credit both to its designer and to owner and builder Mike Searle.

* PFA Chief Engineer.

Chapter 15
Jaguar development flying

At the end of the 1970s the first of the programmes of international collaboration on military aircraft emerged with the Jaguar fighter bomber for France and the United Kingdom. The consortium formed for this, SEPECAT, consisted initially of Breguet Aviation and the British Aircraft Corporation for the airframe and weapons system, and Rolls-Royce and Turbomeca for the Adour engines. Shortly after commencement of the programme however, Breguet were taken over by Avions Marcel Dassault which then headed and managed the French element with the Breguet division continuing as the French design-authority.

The UK responsibility was placed on BAC's military aircraft division at Warton under F.W. Page, with Ivan Yates as project director and Jimmy Dell as project test pilot.

Flight trials were planned on a parallel basis, with the French-built prototype first flown by Bernard Witt at Istres on the Mediterranean coast in 1969, and the second (British-built) aircraft at Warton by Jimmy Dell; with facilities for interchanging test pilots between the bases to ensure continuity of experience. For this programme a heavy commitment was made to providing identical computer capacity at each design centre and also at the test bases, with the combined objects of ensuring rapid progress and of controlling the complexities of the international organization within a strict and workable discipline.

The author after testing a Jaguar at the French test centre at Istres with Breguet test pilot Jesberger.

Left *John Cockburn briefs the author in the front cockpit of a Warton development Jaguar.*

Right *Handing over the first of two Jaguars for the Empire Test Pilot's School.*

This all went well initially and the prototypes made good progress in their test programmes, delayed only by some development problems with the Adour engine; and it began to seem as if this advanced computer-based flight testing system was working according to plan. But then, two years into the test programme, some indications appeared that all was not well. In some of Jimmy Dell's earliest reports from flying at Istres followed by confirmatory tests on Warton aircraft, criticisms had appeared of the lateral control quality and these had continued as experience was gained.

Flight safety was not thought to be involved and no immediate action had been called for pending long-term correction, but as the months went by without corrective actions and as the flight reports continued to record concern, the writer as the director responsible for all flight test programmes at Warton took a close look at the problem and found consistent reported evidence

of unsatisfactory (though not unsafe) lateral control over many months. There was also a measure of agreement in the Warton specialist technical departments that all was not well with the aircraft's roll response to turbulence. Beyond that, nothing: there was in fact a clear blocking element somewhere in the system vetoing any corrective action in this matter, although Warton's aerodynamicists had already schemed a roll-autostabilizer system and shown in their computer and wind tunnel studies that it could, if fully developed, provide a simple and effective answer to the problem.

Although not qualified on Jaguar or by then in current fast-jet practice, the writer had flown the two-seater Jaguar with Jimmy Dell at Istres early in the programme first from the rear seat, and later in command from the front cockpit with Paul Millett as the Jaguar qualified pilot supervising from the back.

The Jaguar was no 'Tiger' to an ex-Lightning

pilot and its simple, pleasant general controllability, albeit within the limitations imposed by high wing loading and modest power-to-weight ratio, had posed no difficulties. What proved to be a surprise however, when coming straight to the point without progressive experience to blunt first impressions, was the contrast throughout most of the flight envelope between the positive and well damped elevator and the quite imprecise and poorly damped spoiler lateral control.

Powerful roll-rate was available as advertised in all conditions, but at some points in the flight envelope damping of small lateral displacements was almost non-existent suggesting imminent pilot-induced oscillation; and the aeroplane had felt generally uneasy in the lateral sense and a long way short of the crisp, firm but responsive platform essentially required of this low-level, high-speed military aircraft. But now, in 1971, there had been no corrective action and the

national authorities had begun to express concern.

Finding at the December 1972 meeting of the Warton board that this matter was not on the agenda although it had been specifically requested, the writer raised it in 'matters arising' and was surprised to find a board-room row on his hands!

The Jaguar directorate categorically denied that any problem existed and stated that there was no evidence. However the Flight Operations Department had done their homework and were able to table relevant references in many flight reports dating back for over two years. Reference was also made to reports that had just come in that official test pilots from Boscombe Down and Centre d'Essai en Vol, the French flight test centre, had encountered 'almost uncontrollable' conditions laterally in tests with centre-line stores in the presence of bad weather turbulence.

The Jaguar office argued that the two cases

were not connected (which in fact they were), and Page cut short the argument and shortly afterwards issued a directive for the trial installation of the optimized roll autostabilizer, which had been under development for some time, to the lateral control spoilers. This modification was test flown successfully as ultimately confirmed by the writer in a flight test report dated 16 February 1973 following a front cockpit flight with John Cockburn in two-seat Jaguar *XW556*.

'Summary. . .

'This brief experience confirmed that throughout the major proportion of the "clean" aircraft flight envelope as covered, controllability with three-axes autostabilization has been improved to a point where it is obviously excellent for the rôle...'

XW556 was flown again for final assessment by the writer from the rear cockpit with Tim Ferguson on 4 April 1973 prior to submission of the roll-stabilizer for Boscombe Down trials, and was reported on in the summary:

'At low level moderate to severe turbulence was encountered and lateral damping assessed at 460kt IAS down to 150ft.

'With roll damper off, lateral damping in gusts was poor to the point of disrupting tracking accuracy, but switching in roll-damper immediately reduced these disturbances to an acceptable level. In these circumstances the aircraft was felt to have fully acceptable characteristics of stability and control for the primary role. . .'

The roll stabilizer was introduced subsequently to the production standard and eliminated this problem; and this incident demonstrated the shortcomings of sole dependence on computer evidence in a flight test programme, and of the continued vital importance of taking note of qualitative assessment by experienced test pilots.

Chapter 16

Tornado test flight

Preparation for flying any modern high performance military aircraft is liable to be a lengthy matter, and the days of five minutes with Pilots' Notes followed by a brief 'run round the cockpit' and then 'kick the tyres and light the fires' are a distant memory. However, the Tornado is no more complex in terms of preparation for flight than were its immediate predecessors. Where it does differ from them is in the advanced weapons system capability which necessitates many weeks of crew-training for the pilot and systems operator to enable them, working as a team, to reach the proficiency level needed to obtain the maximum military potential in all possible circumstances.

Having been involved in the management of the flight development programme since its inception, the author's opportunity to fly an early development Tornado came with the arrival on flight status of the first dual-control prototype, *PO3*, in 1975, as referred to in the following chapter. The specific purpose of this prototype was to establish acceptability of the dual control configuration in general and the suitability of the rear (instructor's) cockpit and vision angles; so specialist training was not needed for a handling assessment from the rear seat, and after an aero-medical briefing on the escape system at Boscombe Down following a professional engineering briefing on it at the well-equipped Warton Safety Equipment section, all was set for the formal pre-flight briefing. This was conducted in Warton's traditional manner by the flight test engineer in charge of the particular aircraft programme together with the aircraft project pilot, both sides supported as necessary by systems, aerodynamics and other specialists involved, including air traffic control.

PO3's project pilot was J.D. Eagles, then Deputy Chief Test Pilot (Executive Director Flight Operations in 1985), who had made the first flight of this prototype earlier in the month.

The briefing covered the scheduled test points in relation to the findings of the previous flight, work done since and the relevant standard of flight limitations including some imposed specifically for this flight; and so to the Operations Room which at Warton is a purpose-developed and staffed operations planning and co-ordinating centre. Here the sortie detail was formally authorized by the Deputy Chief Test Pilot and passed by operations staff to Air Traffic who, by the time *PO3* called the Tower, had established a priority area for the type of tests required. These were to be predominantly over the Irish Sea for all supersonic work, or over the Pennines or Welsh hills for low-level testing.

The test objectives for this sortie were directional and longitudinal stability measurements at subsonic and supersonic speeds and general handling evaluation from the rear cockpit, so a flight plan was cleared for subsonic work on climb to 30,000ft north-west followed by supersonic points over the sea under Warton radar, and then recovery to the Ribble estuary and Warton for low-level handling and circuit work.

The weather was reviewed relative to the local forecast and the latest satellite chart and judged satisfactory by Eagles, and the crew moved out in the Operations radio Land-Rover to the experimental flight shed area on the south side of Warton at the edge of the Ribble estuary. On looking west over the Irish Sea while crossing the main runway, the sky looked good for the planned tests.

Tornado *03* seemed unimpressive on the ground owing to its short fuselage and high

undercarriage — an impression which disappears when airborne with wings swept at 66° when the Tornado looks every inch a fast and efficient military aircraft.

Entry into the rear cockpit (prototype, and not fully representative of the production trainer) was easy as it is spacious and uncongested. When settled into the Mk 10 Martin Baker seat with connectors fastened and harness adjusted, accessibility of controls and most major references was satisfactory, although the battery charger selector (a non-standard prototype fit) was too far to the rear for comfortable operation, and the canopy jettison lever and parking brake lever necessitated stooping and groping under the sills to operate.

Canopy locking proved straightforward, and vision from the rear seat was good in all directions except directly forward where it was obstructed by the pilot's ejection seat. In general the quality of vision at oblique angles through the canopy was unusually good, but two small areas of distortion on this prototype were noted as being unacceptable for production standard. In addition, even with the instructor's seat raised electrically to maximum sitting height it was felt that this would be barely sufficient for instructor vision, but it was noted that a significant margin

existed between the top of the Mk 2 helmet and the canopy to provide for an improved seat-height adjustment range.

Pre-flight control checks were carried out on the auxiliary power unit from the front cockpit before engine starts, and these showed that aft and sideways stick travel was slightly restricted by the instructor's knees and harness QRB (quick release box).

Engine start and run-up procedures for the RB 199 are simple and engine noise at ground-idle scarcely perceptible. At full 'dry' power and in reheat on the ground and subsequently in the air they were exceptionally quiet and smooth, and when operated from the rear cockpit throttles the engine responses were precise, positive and operationally suitable; but *PO3*'s throttle friction loads were considered excessive as they were subsequently in flight at that early stage in the engine programme. On this first trainer the throttle boxes were sub-standard and flown 'on concession', but later in the programme improved production units cured this problem.

Cockpit air-conditioning produced a heavy draught at the 'instructor's' right knee area which caused initial chilling discomfort and much disruption of checklist papers. Development subsequently introduced adjustable 'body sprays'

Left *Paul Millet and Ray Woollett climbing the first British MRCA (Tornado) prototype PO2 over the Cumbrian coast in 1975.*

Right *The author congratulates Pietro Trevison, Aeritalia chief test pilot, on his first Tornado flight with Paul Millet (centre).*

which eliminated this discomfort.

During taxying and take-off by the front seat pilot, instructor vision was limited to that through either of the pilot's quarter-panels, but seemed adequate. However at V_r, all effective forward runway reference from the back seat was lost as is the case with most fast-jet tandem cockpit trainers.

The quiet smoothness of the engines and the firm stability of the airframe was noted in the climb-out, but some airframe roughness was apparent. (This and other areas of roughness were later improved by developments to the rear fuselage configuration.)

After an initial undercarriage locking-up problem had been sorted out, control was taken for the rest of the sortie from the rear cockpit on the climb from 5,000ft, levelling off initially at 11,500ft. At wing 25°, 330kt IAS, controllability from the rear cockpit with full Command and Stability Augmentation System (CSAS) was precise, with responses and dead-beat damping ideal for precision flying. Engine response to throttle in the dry range was ideal with engines quiet and vibration-free, but throttle loads were confirmed as an area for future development.

Wing sweeping from 25° to 66° and back was accompanied by very minor changes in trim, nose down/nose up, which did not need retrimming; but when trimming was first carried out the feel of the trim switch was not liked owing both to slow rate and to the shape of the switch control. Thereafter in the flight however, any retrimming was done without further criticism, so this was a learning-curve case. System jolts were noticed with initiation and completion of each sweep operation, but not to a significant extent which would need development action.

On increasing wing-sweep angle between 45° and 66° at 330kt IAS/11,000ft, a change in airflow noise level occurred. This did not alter up to 400kt IAS, but at 66°/Mach 0.85/450kt IAS the noise level changed again to a higher note. Pulling $2\frac{1}{2}$g here resulted in increase of roughness suggesting a flow separation on top of the canopy; and the pitch stick-force required was considered undesirably heavy for this moderate manoeuvre. Response and damping were precise in all axes. Again these criticisms were improved or eliminated in subsequent development.

In these flight conditions the 'instructor's' view was good all round, except in a 30° cone directly ahead blanked by the pilot's seat. The two rear-view mirrors were thought to be limited in operational value to checking formating aircraft and one's own contrail, and it was noted that in

Roll-out of the first production series Tornado GT001 from the West German factory at Manching on 6 June 1979, the day following the first British production Tornado BT001 roll-out at Warton.

maximum dry a dense black trail was visible in the mirrors (a problem totally eliminated in later-standard production engines).

Handling at 520kt IAS/Mach 0.98 in 66° sweep continued to show extreme precision with full CSAS. Selection to Direct Link (first failure — DL) resulted in reduction in damping and crispness of response in pitch and roll, but still provided adequate controllability in normal manoeuvring. Airframe roughness increased to sharp-edged at Mach 0.98 and then was eliminated in transition to Mach 1.02 which was reached without trim change or other disturbance (full CSAS).

A Mach 0.9 climb was resumed to 30,000ft and the well-damped stability and precision of control was fully appreciated in IMC (instrument meteorological conditions). In handling at 26–30,000ft some buffet was noticeable at 1g/Mach 0.99/410kt IAS, although this was again transitory, reducing below Mach 0.95 and disappearing above Mach 1.0. Recovery in part-IMC from 17,000ft to the Warton circuit was

again exceptional for its ease and precision at varying wing sweep angles and over a speed range of 550–250kt IAS.

In low-level handling with full CSAS at 350–450kt IAS, wing 66°, controllability in reverse turns to 3g, wing-overs and 360°/1g rolls was virtually ideal, with the exception of the longitudinal stick force gradient which was considered rather steep for operational low-level manoeuvring.

Throughout the flight the absence of a slip-ball in the rear cockpit had proved no embarrassment, with full CSAS apparently holding slip-ball central in the front cockpit in all manoeuvres — a directionally stiff aeroplane with dead-beat damping.

Circuit flying from the rear cockpit in the visual pattern proved straightforward with 200kt IAS downwind and 160 on finals. With the instructor's view ahead limited to through one or other of the front quarter panels, offset into a strong crosswind can result in loss of view of the runway behind the windscreen arch, and this had to be considered when setting up the final approach.

On short finals at 11–12 units ADD* (angle of attack sensor) there was just sufficient vision to judge the flare, but once completed direct forward runway vision was lost until the nosewheel was lowered to contact. Three axes stability and control responses, and also speed stability were most marked in establishing the aircraft on base leg and finals, and the aircraft was landed gently from the back seat at the author's first attempt. At no time was the instructor's stick felt to be too short for comfort (ref a previous criticism) but even at maximum sitting height the rear seat was always a little too low.

The author's flight report from this early flight on *PO3*, Flight 7, Schedule 7, 13 August 1975, included the following:

'Within the flight envelope areas experienced:

'a) Exceptional precision and controllability with full CSAS.

'b) Adequate controllability in Direct Link.

'c) Good instructor's station and ability to land from this position.

'd) Good and entirely acceptable engine control characteristics, with low noise and vibration levels.

'It is already at this early stage an exceptional aeroplane which looks well set to achieve its specific targets.'

There were also some less complimentary comments on a lateral pilot-induced oscillation incident, and on the general level of airframe buffet roughness at that stage which was compared unfavourably with a Lightning; but these problem areas were eventually eliminated for the final excellent production standard.

---

* Measure of aircraft attitude relative to airflow in the high-lift or landing configuration.

Chapter 17

Tornado flight development

The Jaguar programme was not alone in demonstrating weaknesses in over-dependence on computer technology in flight testing.

The trinational 'Panavia' management of the design, construction and development of the Tornado was monitored and not always helped by an additional management body called 'NAMMA' representing the three customer national governments of West Germany, Italy and the United Kingdom. This produced a management pyramid with NAMMA overseeing Panavia who in turn co-ordinated the programme activities of the three technical and commercial giants, Messerschmitt Bolkow Blohm, Aeritalia (Fiat) and British Aerospace. Through this bureaucratic jungle Panavia had to establish and control a cohesive policy and run a programme to produce the West's potentially most complex and effective all-weather low-level strike aircraft, all within a strict cost and time schedule.

It says much for the dedication of the Panavia international team drawn from the three companies, and for the outstanding capability of Professor Gero Madelung, the first Panavia managing director, that the many and massive problems arising were overcome by 1979 when, with the first production aircraft, a suitable standard had been achieved for introduction into the three services — though with some initial limitations and not without some unplanned arisings in no way dissimilar to those of the pre-computer era.

In the first year of test flying the basic control and stability of this not very graceful, short-coupled variable geometry aeroplane proved sufficiently safe and controllable to enable the flight envelope to be expanded on schedule into the high Mach and high IAS regions firstly without and then with external stores, and so on into the vitally important area of high incidence and stalling and spinning. Also, the complex electronic and hydraulic systems showed admirable reliability and were not a serious holding feature. Only the RB199 engine proved a delaying factor with surge-line problems constraining the rate of test progress on the aeroplane for a number of years.

This was yet another example of the delays to be expected and which should be planned for when a new engine design is specified for a new aircraft. Two to three years' 'lead-time' is essential before a new basic engine can be expected to give reliable flight-running free of repetitive defects or handling problems; but in the case of the Tornado the RB199 engine design was not 'frozen' until more than one year after the aircraft's initial contract was placed, inevitably with consequent delays to the urgent flight development programme accompanied by the time-wasting mutual misunderstandings and acrimony between the engine and aircraft manufacturers which tend to occur in these circumstances.

Apart from these issues, two main areas of concern in the Tornado design phase had been the advanced avionics and electronics and, of course, the variable geometry wing. Design leadership for the latter had been placed with British Aircraft Corporation Military Aircraft Division at Warton under Ray Creasey, who had for many years specialized in developing the VG theories of Barnes Wallis of Vickers.

Avionics design was in the competent hands of Messerschmitt Bolkow Blohm, who set about the demanding requirement for the Tornado's 'Command and Stability Augmentation System' (CSAS) with determination and enthusiasm — so much so in fact that when the first definitive statement on the system was circulated within the Panavia group of companies, Warton Flight Operations noted with amused disbelief that among the long list of 'modes' for the integrated autopilot was one for 'Formation'! Avionics specialists at Warton, when questioned, merely confirmed with a slight lift of the eyebrows — what were 'the pilots' complaining about now!

Further investigation did indeed reveal an earnest professor beavering away in splendid isolation deep in the Messerschmitt empire at Munich, totally dedicated to the idea that the Tornado was an aeroplane of such complexity and demanding performance requirements that 'the pilots would be unable to cope with formation flying in addition to everything else'! So he was going to provide them with an immensely complex Auto-Formation-Flying facility at great cost to the programme which was, of course, well known to be not lacking in funds. Questions of whether he had based his assumptions on operational advice and, if so, by whom, were never answered; but operationally there was no case for such a system and eventually through the slow-moving official channels the 'Auto Formation' mode was cancelled.

Two years after the first flight of the prototype, which had been carried out successfully at Manching Ingolstadt in August 1974 by BAC's Paul Millett and MBB's Nils Meister, concern was being expressed by some of the test pilots about some aspects of the lateral control.

The CSAS was already becoming renowned for its precision of control over a wide range of conditions in the demanding flight envelope, and pilots' reports had frequently expressed approval of the superior control qualities from low speed/high angles of attack right through to 800kt IAS and Mach 2.0. Particularly impressive also was the auto-safeguarding provided by the system which would allow the pilot to pull limit g at maximum roll-stick deflection at limit speed without overstressing or reaching an out-of-control condition. This was the first known military aircraft ever to have a 'fail-safe' control system, although the RAF's English Electric Lightning could be said to have this capability over a substantial part of its performance envelope.

At an increasing rate from the end of 1975 however, comments were made by test pilots about occasional lack of precise lateral control in the final phase of the approach and flare before touchdown. It was thought that turbulence and crosswinds might be factors in this, but measured evidence from the on-board computers with air-to-ground data transmission by telemetry was inconclusive. Computer and simulator studies had shown margins from lateral pilot-induced oscillation to be small, but no smaller than already existed on in-service types such as the Phantom; and on the apparent assumption that this was a valid comparison no action was being proposed by the design authority.

A sharp division of opinion now became apparent. Some members of Warton Flight Operations and some Warton aerodynamicists believed that a major problem existed with the CSAS lateral computer, which they said, was over-sensitive or 'too high-gain'. Their Italian counterparts at Aeritalia Turin agreed with this, but the MBB element at Munich who had design and financial responsibility stated firmly 'no evidence', although some of their test pilots voiced doubts informally.

The co-ordinating international programme management Panavia in this instance did not want to know. Earlier in 1974 the writer, as the test programme director, had decided to take a personal look as soon as this was practical; and when the first dual-control prototype, *PO3*, made its first flight in August 1975 at Warton flown by BAC deputy chief test pilot Dave Eagles, a few days later with Eagles in command the writer flew a sortie in it from the back seat as described in the previous chapter.

This was instructive in many ways, confirming the suitability of the instructor's station in the rear cockpit and the by any standards remarkable precision of the CSAS through the performance envelope, especially in relation to the wing-sweep angle which could even be varied stick-free with hardly any noticeable change in longitudinal trim. Returning to Warton for a practice approach and overshoot, this proved so straightforward from the back seat that the writer landed gently first time and then Eagles from the front seat took over to climb out initially for another circuit and landing by the writer.

This time with a strong crosswind the writer in the back became unsighted ahead and overshot the approach centre-line, and Eagles took over to complete a necessary sharp side-step manoeuvre to regain the centre-line.

This all seemed smooth and normal until, as Eagles flared the Tornado gently over the runway threshold marks, suddenly the stick began to thrash violently laterally to full travel each way and hit the writer's knees in the back cockpit.

Briefly the aircraft was felt to go out of phase with the stick. Then, still level at 5–6 ft and in ground-effect, Eagles released and steadied the stick, the oscillation stopped and the Tornado touched down as if nothing had happened.

The incident had occurred with a lightly loaded aircraft in hardly any turbulence and in fine weather. With underwing stores on a dark night or in turbulent bad weather, it seemed to the writer that it could probably have been much more severe and even catastrophic. But despite increasingly urgent recommendations from Flight Operations over a long period, no formal corrective action was taken; although it was known by 1978 that in the rarefied atmosphere of MBB's avionics department far removed from the political centre of Panavia, action had been in hand for some time to develop software for a modification to the existing 'Mk 5' lateral computer to reduce its 'gain' and to improve its margins against PIO.

Ultimately in late 1978, with still no practical action in sight the writer decided that the issue must be raised formally and looking for support found the Italian technical director in favour, the West German opposed and the British colleague slightly half-hearted. At this point when Warton technical opinion at working level was seen to be clearly in favour of modification, the Warton technical director eventually gave what appeared to be assurance of support if 'Flight Operations' would make a formal recommendation.

This action was tabled at the next management board in Munich at which the new chairman (with a financial and non-technical background) and his technical deputy were less than enthusiastic and tended towards accepting MBB's renewed statement of 'no evidence'. The Flight Operations case was made unequivocally that there was indeed sufficient evidence for concern that not only was the lateral control inadequate when judged qualitatively in relation to the severe operating requirements of the specification, but also that the customer authorities, especially the British MOD

Procurement Executive, would be most likely to reject the current standard and refuse to accept delivery, if unmodified, of the first production aircraft.

This caused a stirring of interest amongst the accountants present, but the final important support which would be vital to sway the argument if it was put to the vote was not forthcoming and, in what seemed at first to start as a supportive statement, the Warton technical director suddenly changed direction and ended up perched squarely on the fence!

The chairman refused to make a ruling and again referred the matter back to the technical departments, but the author stated that action was now essential if production deliveries to 'initial operating clearance' (IOC) were not to be seriously delayed, and said that the national authorities would have to be informed. This produced some action, and within a week Panavia circulated full go-ahead instructions for the modified lateral computer to be clearance-tested and introduced into production as the 'Mk 8L' standard; but this was coupled with a stricture from the Panavia chairman that the 'Flight Operations' case had been 'slanted'!

Only to the extent that it had been solely aimed at achieving a safe standard for the Tornado's introduction to the three nations' air forces was this true, and once again these events highlighted the vital importance of retaining the ability of test pilots to give reliable qualitative appraisals.

Vast computer capacity shows no sign of enabling an aeroplane to be designed without fault or the need to develop out inevitable defects. In every case in the final analysis, while man is required to control the vehicle whether he is called 'Pilot', 'Systems Manager', 'Computer Controller' or just plain 'Captain', it is man the Test Pilot who alone can define if the final integrated result of all those years of endeavour by thousands of dedicated engineers with their megabanks of computer power, is safe and practical to fly.

When subsequently introduced into service with the NATO air forces, the Tornado quickly proved to be the most effective military aircraft of its category in the world, and in the process won the two top awards in the USAF bombing competitions against all contenders in 1985 and again in 1986.

Conclusion

Forty years of RAF and industry flying could not fail to leave some indelible impressions.

Firstly, the Royal Air Force. Without question the world's finest air force in 1940 and still, though small by comparison with many others, the finest in quality today. It was a proud privilege to serve in Fighter Command for the seven years encompassing World War 2, and the standards of integrity, responsibility and discipline with humour demanded without question in those times, set a pattern for the future which seems even more desirable and relevant to the troubled times of 1986.

Then the industry. Often the butt of political abuse, the aircraft industry of this country has proved time-and-again that it is able to lead the world in innovative design; but its best endeavours have too often been frustrated by political cancellation, or by endless official indecision in the placing of contracts for essential re-equipment until too late when overseas purchase then becomes inevitable to meet the vital needs of defence.

Finally the test pilot. Though often in the past portrayed as some white-overalled 'Ace-from-the-Base', and in more recent times as a somewhat humourless, over-professional sub-astronaut, the test pilot remains an integral and vital part in the great team effort needed to hone to a fine edge the ultimate instrument; the complex and capable modern aeroplane. Without his skills, judgement and dedication, even in today's computerized world the aeroplane cannot be made safe; and management environments must continue to be evolved in which the voice of the experienced experimental test pilot can be heard at policy level.

The computer will not replace the test pilot while manned air and space vehicles are still required. He is here to stay.

Appendix 1 — A policy for display flying

Copy memorandum.
'British Aircraft Corporation, Flight Operations, Warton, 1971

'Techniques for demonstration flying.
'Some thoughts for the 1971 season.

'Reference is often made to the "art of demonstration flying" as if it was some form of activity far removed from practical aviation and requiring special, even slightly supernatural powers, of the pilot. That this is a misjudgement is sometimes not appreciated even by pilots themselves, but good demonstration flying is a matter largely of hard work and persistence in practice.

'The reason for demonstration flying is generally to show an influential person or group that the new aeroplane (i) actually flies, (ii) flies interestingly, (iii) flies to specification, (iv) does it all better than the opposition.

'Therefore from the beginning it is necessary to compare performance and handling characteristics with those of the competition so as to concentrate on any areas of obvious advantage such as STOL, turning manoeuvrability, rate of roll, slow flying, etc.

'Attention must be given to preparing the aircraft to a standard which will give the pilot the best chance of achieving a clean display of the planned programme.

'This will involve review of fuel state, external stores, engine settings and reliability especially if experimental reheat systems are involved, wheel and parachute braking systems, tyre pressures, flying controls and auto-stabilizer systems, cabin conditioning and windscreen demist/rain blow systems, and the cockpit layout where vital instrument references may need to be moved into "line of sight" for critical low flying, such as AOA*, etc. In short all possible areas where attention to detail may improve the ability of the pilot to achieve an attractive performance.

'Only when the best possible demonstration

* AOA = Angle of attack

standard has been established — and it invariably is not ideal — can the pilot set about planning the flying.

'In public displays the time allowance is generally restrictive, and the only way to get the best out of a 4–5 minute slot is to work out and practise a sequence that fits; and here the skill and knowledge of the pilot (or lack of it) becomes very apparent. Even with military aircraft the majority of general flying must obviously be conducted under the rigid rules of planned procedure in controlled airspace, or out of it under radar surveillance; and very little time can be obtained for genuinely unrestricted low flying practice. Yet in demonstration the pilot is required to haul high performance, highly loaded equipment around the close confines of an airfield sufficiently tightly to stay in sight of the spectators and at very low levels.

'In public displays it is easy to see which pilots are up to it and which are not, and a change of pilots can sometimes be seen to change the character of the display of a particular aircraft significantly.

'Therefore, since the sole object of demonstration flying is to show the aircraft in the best possible light, the pilot must be able to get the best out of it with safety.

'This is only possible with knowledge and practice — knowledge of where the limitations are at all significant points in the flight envelope and systems operations, and sufficient practice under simulated demonstration conditions for the pilot to be able to recognize instantly the physical warnings such as buffet boundary, stall boundary, adverse yaw, engine surge, etc, and their significance relative to the planned flight sequence.

'It can be embarrassing for example if "yaw-off" is not recognized in a "rotation" climb on a Lightning when committed in an 80° climb at 230kt/1,000ft, or a wing drop in a 90° bank on a Canberra at 200kt/200ft — but if the pilot is fully "current" in these conditions he can fly safely to the limits where, if he did not know the aircraft properly, he would have to loosen up the pattern which would then be immediately recognizable from the ground.

'Once the appropriate level of knowledge of the aircraft and skill has been acquired, a sequence must be worked out with the object of demonstrating throughout the entire time-slot from brakes-off right through to the end of the landing run. The days of the improvisers are past, and the best of them were never up to the pilots who planned and practised their programmes.

'In planning a demonstration the factors to be considered are:-

'1. State of the aircraft relative to limitations and reliability of systems.
'2. Any particular feature lending itself to demonstration — ie, power/weight ratio, low wing loading, STOL, etc.
'3. Any feature not necessarily associated with ·(2) but required to be shown for sales purposes.
'4. Potential of any competition, ie, if *they* fly with external stores, you may have to.
'5. Layout and local topography of display airfield.
'6. Integration with preceding and succeeding aircraft — ie, useful extra time can often be obtained by mutal agreement to overlap.
'7. Finally, the choice and sequence of manoeuvres. With the standard rules which apply at most public displays restricting flight over or towards the crowd, there is an inevitable tendency for each item to become a standard "Dumbells"; but with ingenuity and effort this can be overcome, more easily of course with low wing loading types than with the higher loadings.

'Here is where precise knowledge of the aircraft characteristics is essential. For example a supersonic aircraft making a fast pass at the display limit at 0.95 and breaking into a decelerating turn for a slow run, can use up most of its allotted time doing just this. Whereas if, for example, in a Lightning the pilot pulls limit g all the way round the deceleration until lighting the burners and hitting the critical thrust boundary balance point at about 4g/290kt, he can then hold a minimum radius 360° at max reheat, controlling speed solely on elevator by varying the induced drag, and come back in for a roll or wing-over into the approach, all within the time-slot and staying right in front of the audience — but it needs practice to get the "break" condition and position right, and if the pilot was not able to recognize the "yaws" when sustaining an 80–90° bank under these conditions at 150ft or so above ground level, the results could be spectacular.

'To summarize:-

'1. Get the aeroplane into the best possible condition for the purpose.
'2. Know the limitations from experience of frequent practice at low level.
'3. Never under any circumstances try and improvise during a display with a manoeuvre you've never practised before — this continues to happen, sometimes disastrously and often with near disastrous results when pilots have gone beyond test limits and extended the current envelope in the process!
'4. Take all precautions possible against known risk elements, ie, don't accept down-wind landings with a high performance aircraft just because ATC would like it that way.
'5. Make every second of your show count by flying on "your" limits all the time and continuously tightening it up. It is only by so doing that your aircraft can be made to look different and eye-catching, and a "loose" show is not worth watching.
'6. Have a contingency "fill-in" sequence rehearsed so as to take immediate advantage of an invitation to extend your time, as sometimes happens in a public display, without wandering round the sky looking lost.
'7. Always be prepared to adapt your planned pattern to weather, ie, down-wind fast — upwind slow — unlike the pilot of a high performance entry at a recent international display who resolutely made his "slow" landing-configuration pass each day down a 30–35kt prevailing wind and his "fast" run up it!

'8. Confidence and fine judgement in low flying only comes with practice and this is traditionally difficult to obtain formally. But there is often a chance for a few low passes at the end of a test sortie, and display pilots should make opportunities for authorized practice in this way on every suitable occasion throughout the year — critics who may be heard to complain about "showing off" and "unnecessary low flying" can generally be expected to be the first to complain about uninspired demonstrations!

'9. To prepare a high performance military aircraft for one display flight can cost many thousands of pounds, and however good the aeroplane is its showing can be rendered dull by inadequate flying or counter-productive by dangerous flying.

'Consistently good demonstrations can improve the chances of sales — and this is what we are here for.

'R.P. Beamont
Director'

Appendix 2

'RAF Exeter. No 10 Group, Fighter Command — Combat Report.

'Sector Serial No ....
'Serial No of Order detailing
'Flight or Squadron to Patrol .... (B) 82
'Date .... (C) 25/8/40
Flight, Squadron .... (D) Flight B, Sqdn 87
'Number of Enemy Aircraft .... (E) 100+
'Type of Enemy Aircraft .... (F) Ju 88 Do 17 Me 109
'Time Attack was delivered .... (G) 17.30
'Place Attack was delivered .... (H) six miles NE Portland
Height of Enemy .... (J) 11,000ft
Enemy Casualties .... (K) 1 Me 109 (Cat 1)
                                                                                                    1 Do 17   (Cat 2)

'Our Casualties .... Aircraft .... (L) —
                                                  Personnel .... (M) —
'Searchlights ....   N/A
'Was enemy illuminated? If not were they in front or   N/A
behind the target (N) 1 AA Guns.   N/A
'Did shell bursts assist pilot in intercepting the enemy   (N) II — shell bursts indicated
                                                                                               direction of raid towards
                                                                                               Portland.

'GENERAL REPORT. We attacked the main bomber formation from 1,000ft above and out of the sun. I fired a long burst from the beam at a Do 17, closing to fifty yards and the EA turned on its back with smoke pouring out and dived towards the sea. At 5,000ft I engaged an Me 109 and after some minutes forced it down into a field between Abbotsbury and Weymouth and about one mile inland. The pilot appeared unhurt and set fire to his machine.

'Signature: R.P. Beamont P/O
W.D. David F/O OC ⎰   Flight B
P.S. Mills S/L OC ⎱ Squadron 87'

Appendix 3

'RAF Manston Intelligence Reports on the first night ground attacks by Typhoons.

'FINAL INTRUDER REPORT — 609 SQUADRON, R.A.F. MANSTON, KENT. NIGHT OF 17/18 NOV. 1942

'1 Typhoon Ib, 609 West Riding Squadron (S/L Beamont DFC), left Manston 2020 hours for Intruder Operation Berck-Abbeville-Amiens. Possible targets: trains, barges, or E/A over Amiens-Glisy aerodrome. Crossing English coast at Dungeness, he crossed Channel climbing to 8,000ft. Weather was 10/10ths cloud at 2,000ft over Channel, extending to two miles inland, which effectually prevented opposition from S/Ls or Flak on making landfall at Berck at 6,000ft. Between this point and Abbeville, where 10/10ths cloud and fog began, weather was clear moonlight except for ground haze. After proceeding at 3,000ft via Somme estuary along the Somme-Abbeville canal, where no activity was seen, S/L Beamont turned and found a train proceeding towards coast between Port-le-Grand and Doyelles-sur-Mer, and consisting mainly of box-like coaches. He made 5 right-angle attacks opening fire at 500/1,000ft and pulling out at 50/100ft, and firing an average burst of 2½–3 secs. After the second attack the train halted and the locomotive was enveloped in steam. From the middle of the train intermittent dull-red explosions were seen both during and after attack. On breaking away from the first two attacks, S/L Beamont passed over St Valerie-sur-Somme, where a searchlight illuminated him and held him for 0–2,500ft despite evasive action, to the accompaniment of accurate fire from 4 Bofors guns in the same position. During subsequent attacks this position was avoided. After the last attack S/L Beamont re-crossed coast at Berck at 5,000ft and landed at Manston at 2125. Time over target: 2045–2105.

'Points of Interest
'1.   Plotting lights which followed, but were not necessarily beneath.
'2.   A semi-obscured winking orange glow seen from inland, apparently on a hill near Lancheres.
'3.   A yellow searchlight in Boulogne area, with red self-destroying tracer going up beam and bursting yellow.
'4.   Three bomb bursts between Boulogne and Calais.
'5.   Slight difficulty was experienced during initial stages of each attack in getting sight on to target owing to ground haze and narrow vertical angle of vision of Typhoon aircraft.

'(Sgd)   F.H. ZIEGLER
Flying Officer
Intelligence Officer,
No. 609 WR Squardron

'Distribution:

Station Commander, BIGGIN HILL
Station Commander, MANSTON
W/C Gleed, H.Q.F.C.
W/C Walker, HQ No 11 Group
Senior Controller, "Intruder" Ops'

Appendix 4

'RAF Manston 11 Group Fighter Command Combat Report.'

[The first daylight ground-attack sortie by Typhoons.]

'To: HQ 11 Group (R) Hornchurch
'From: Manston
'MI/7 13/12 COMPOSITE RHUBARB REPORT 13/12/42
'(A) 609 (B) 2 Typhoons (C) 1449–1545 (D) Amiens-Abbeville Rly, Glisy A/D. (E) 15 minutes.
(F) 3 locomotives Cat B and rolling stock damaged (G) Nil.
'GENERAL: 5 bursts 'friendly' medium ack ack 100yd behind on crossing coast out to sea at
800ft between Folkestone and Dungeness. Made landfall Cayeux 1502 hours at 6,000ft cloud
10/10 at 5/6,000ft, higher inland, with some showers, vis 30/40 miles. Flew at 5,000ft to W of
Abbeville, reconnoitred Drucat A/D from W, nothing seen. S/L Beamont attacked train with large
engine, 10 open and 2 closed trucks headed W on Abbeville-Le Treport line at 660826 (sheet
9D/4). Fired 4 second burst in dive from 1,600–100ft. Strikes observed on trucks, then on engine,
which stopped with bright flash and erupting steam. F/O Lallemand (Belgian) also fired short
burst, but did not press home attack as train already immobilised. S/L Beamont then returned,
cockpit door having opened in dive. F/O Lallemand continued W, and between 2 reservoirs at
Ancheville (540758 sheet 9D/6) attacked engine and tender. Fired several short bursts from
1,000–50ft, saw strikes and steam. Proceeding W, F/O Lallemand saw goods train going S
between Greny and Auquemesnil (400690 sheet 9D/5). Fired short bursts at 1,000 and 50ft, saw 5
strikes second burst, but shooting difficult owing stoppages on 3 cannons. Saw personnel on
believed Derchigny a/d running for blister hangars, and experienced light flak thence. Looking
back saw steam from last engine attacked. Recrossed coast on Berneval at 3,000ft. Films exposed
by both pilots — 1720A.'

Appendix 5

'FINAL INTRUDER REPORT
'609 WEST RIDING SQUADRON, R.A.F. MANSTON. 21/22ND NOV. 1942'

'1 Typhoon IB (S/Ldr Beamont DFC) t/o Manston 2115 for Intruder to Abbeville-Amiens area, and to attack trains. Crossed coast over Le Touquet at 2128 at 7,000ft diving through small break in cloud about 10 miles inland. On way to Abbeville saw train between Le Crotoy and Noyelles but did not attack. At 2140 near Conde-Folie a second train of goods wagons was attacked strikes being seen along the wagons. Patrol continued to Amiens, where blackout was noted to be very bad, many windows being left uncurtained. No activity at Glisy so returned to Abbeville, seeing a train near Hangest-sur-Somme, with engine emitting steam, but on approach of Intruder train shut off steam and was lost. Arrived over Abbeville area at 2210, flying at 300ft with navigation lights on and reconnoitred Drucat, but saw no activity or aircraft. On crossing marshalling yards had noticed a long stationary train to which Intruder returned and attacked from 50ft, engine emitting much steam. Returned and made second attack from same height, when engine tender burst into flames and engine disappeared in clouds of smoke and steam which could be seen in an ascending column 250ft high from Le Crotoy. A second engine was also hit and emitted much steam and 4 lines of goods wagons were also attacked, using up all cannon observing strikes on all rows. By this time about 10 Bofors had opened up at low angle from N.E. of Abbeville, so returned home, crossing out over Hardelot at 5,000ft at 2220 landing at base at 2230.

'*Weather:* Cloud base at coast 2,500ft, top 7,000, 10/10. Inland base 2,000 top 3,000 9/10. Visibility — moderate.

'*Note:* S/Ldr Beamont found that light of bursting cannon shells on lines was very useful in illuminating target and was able to correct his aim. He also notes that low-level attack of this type makes trains stand out very well against the landscape.

'*Second sortie*
'1 Typhoon IB (S/Ldr Beamont DFC) t/o Manston 0013 for anti-train operations in Lille area. Crossed coast over Mardyck at 0023 at 8,000ft diving to 800. At 0028 saw a stationary train, very long heading N composed of low flat trucks, believed to be an ammunition train. Attacked twice, each time receiving Bofors fire from truck immediately behind engine tender. Strikes were seen on the trucks, attacks being made from 100–80ft. Weather conditions further inland made attempt to reach Lille impossible, so turned S.W., and flew to Le Touquet via Hazebrouck and St Omer. At Le Touquet asked for a vector, and crossed coast at approx 0048 at 10,000ft landing at Manston at 0100 hrs. While in vicinity of St Omer saw what appeared to be a house on fire. No S/Ls or flak (other than from the train).

'*Weather:* 20 miles off coast 4/10 cloud base 2,000 increasing to 10/10 top at 7,000. Inland 10/10 top 10,000 descending to 300 in sleet showers, icing throughout. Area Mardyck-Hazebrouck-Ostende slightly clearer.
'*Note:* S/Ldr Beamont is certain that the fire from train was Bofors and not Oerlikon, bursts being seen at approx 8,000ft being red in colour. Fire was not opened up until Intruder had just passed over, ie, from immediately behind.

'R.C. TREWEEKS
P/O
For Station Intelligence Officer
R.A.F. Station, Manston, Kent.'

Appendix 6

'FINAL INTRUDER REPORT
'609 WEST RIDING SQUADRON, R.A.F. MANSTON. 22/23 NOV. 1942

'1 Typhoon IB (S/Ldr Beamont) t/o Manston 2050 as Intruder to Abbeville-Amiens area. Crossed to French coast (via Lympne) over Boulogne/Alprech at 2105 and proceeded to Rue. At 2112 sighted a small goods train moving south between Rue and Romaines consisting of 10 goods wagons, which stopped on approach of Intruder and shut off steam. Intruder attacked four times seeing engine and wagons hit, diving from 1,000, opening fire at 500ft down to 50ft from 3–400yd. Engine emitted steam from both sides, front, underneath and driver's cabin, steam also seen coming from centre of train and guard's van. Two recces were carried out from 200ft 100yd away from train. At 2125 Intruder left train for base as weather was closing in at base, proceeding 15 mile inland to E of Hardelot, where coast was crossed, landing at 2153 hours.

'1 S/L was seen at Le Touquet on way in, and a flickering light like a fire was observed from the direction of Abbeville.

'Weather: Over channel haze up to 3–4,000ft, cloud 5/10 at 2,000 over French coast, 2 miles inland 10/10 at 5,000, 800ft thick, slight haze below. Visibility quite good.

'R.C. TREWEEKS
P/O
For Station Intelligence Officer
R.A.F. Station, Manston, Kent.'

Appendix 7

'RAF Manston. No 11 Group Fighter Command
'Intelligence Reports.
'TO: HQ 11 Group Hornchurch — Swingate — V.A. Dover.
'FROM: Manston
'M1/10 4/4/43 COMPOSITE RAMROD 46 REPORT 4/4/43.
'(A) 137 SQDN and 609 SQDN (B) 8 WHIRLIBOMBERS★ and 9 TYPHOONS 1B (C) 1816/1940 (D) ABBEVILLE MARSHALLING YARDS (E) 1855 HRS (F) ONE FLAK SHIP CAT 11 SHARED BY F/LT WELLS AND F/O EVANS AND ONE R-BOAT CAT 11 AND ONE R-BOAT CAT 111 SHARED BY S/LDR BEAMONT, ADJ PILOT BLANCO (BELGIAN), F/O RAW, F/O CAMERON AND F/O VAN LIERDE (BELGIAN). (G) ONE TYPHOON CAT B PILOT UNINJURED.

'GENERAL: The Manston formation rendezvoused with 2 Spit Sqdns from Hornchurch at Hastings at 500ft at 1830 hrs. French coast crossed at Cayeux Whirlibombers 8,500ft. Typhoons 8,000ft and behind. Target bombed diving from 12,500 to 7,000ft, 16 × 500lbs: inst G.P. 4 bombs seen to burst centre of target and one on large building to the left. Other unobserved.

★ Westland Whirlwind twin-engined fighter-bombers.

A frame from PR-G's gun camera during 609's attack on four 'R' type minesweepers and escort flak ships on 4 April 1943.

Formation recrossed French coast Cayeux 7,000ft and bombers returned escorted by 2 Typhoons after No 609 Sqdn when half way over channel were vectored by Swingate direct to special target (controller P/O Manning). 6 R-boats seen in pairs, line astern towing paravanes travelling in towards Boulogne 4 miles off coast. Inshore of last pair one believed small motor flak ship. Pilots report R-boats appeared to have more than normal complement aboard. S/Ldr Beamont manoeuvred Sqdn to attack down sun. All a/c made one attack each on last pair of R-boats or flak ship. Boats appeared to be taken by surprise and only opened intense return fire especially from flak ship after attack commenced. One Typhoon hit in rudder and one in engine. Flak ship and R-boat seen on fire and strikes on other R-boat. S/Ldr Beamont saw a large object fall off R-boat during his attack. Bandits reported by Hornchurch so leader ordered Squadron home landing just after Whirlibombers. During attack leading R-boats made for Boulogne. Heavy flak accurate for height out to port on entering from position 1 mile S of St Valery-sur-Somme. Over (bombing) target light flak at 5,000ft, some heavy fairly accurate during attack. Weather no cloud visibility 25 miles. Cine camera guns exposed. Ammo expired 2,450rds HEI.AP and S.A.P.I.*'

---

* High Explosive Incendiary, Armour Piercing and Semi-Armour Piercing Incendiary.

Appendix 8

'*RAF Newchurch No 150 Wing 11 Group Fighter Command*
'*Combat Report.*
PILOTS: W/C R BEAMONT DSO DFC & Bar. P/O SLADE-BETTS, F/S McKERRAS, F/S
         FOSTER, F/S DOMANSKI (Polish) 150 Wing 28th May 1944

'At 16.55 hours nine Tempests V of 3 Sqdn took off for CORMEILLE-EN-VEIN Airfield, as
information had been received that FW.190's and Me.410's were seen on a P.R.U. sortie that
morning. Owing to a variety of technical troubles 4 of the Tempests came back before reaching
the French coast. The remaining pilots closed up to loose formation with W/C Beamont leading, a
section to port, P/O Slade-Betts and F/Sgt McKerras, and a section to starboard, F/Sgt Foster and
F/Sgt Domanski.

'They crossed in at AULT at 8,000ft and went straight to CORMEILLE-EN-VEIN passing to
the right of the airfield. In bays on the east side of the south dispersal five T/E aircraft were seen,
so W/C Beamont led the formation into a diving turn out of the sun, opening fire at about 470
ASI, range about 800yd. The W/C's attack was from $\frac{3}{4}$ head on and his target and those of the
other two sections were identified as Ju 88's, possibly Ju 188, painted black all over.

'In the turn and dive P/O Slade-Betts and F/Sgt McKerras had pulled over to starboard but got
into position and P/O Slade-Betts took the aircraft in the bay on the right of the W/C's target, and
F/Sgt McKerras took the next on the right, both observing strikes.

'F/Sgt Foster came down behind W/C Beamont, but as his windshield was oiled up he could not
select a target and fired a very short burst at the same target as the leader. F/Sgt Domanski came

Frames from Tempest V JN751's gun camera showing hits on a Ju 188 near Paris on 28 May 1944.

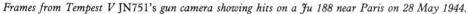

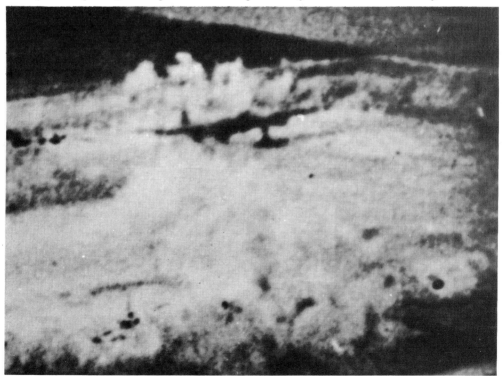

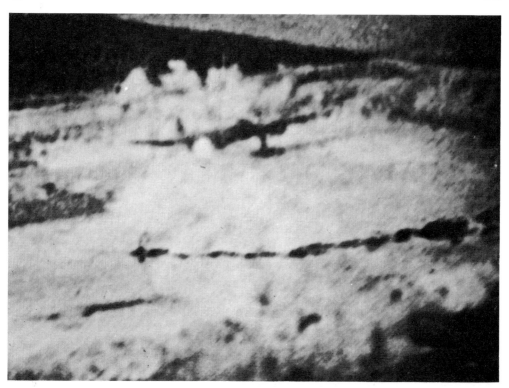

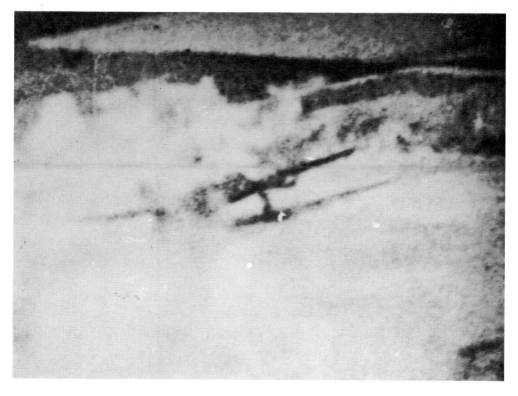

down last, and picking the next aircraft on the right not previously attacked, gave it a burst, observing strikes.

'As W/C Beamont pulled away he saw a piece of his target fly off and the aircraft burning, and F/Sgt Domanski saw this and another target burning. As he crossed the E dispersal, F/Sgt McKerras gave a burst at some huts and saw strikes.

'It was only as the section was at the intersection of the runway that inaccurate fire was opened by light guns. The formation stayed low down for 2 or 3 miles and then climbed. Smoke from two fires was seen from the target up to a distance of six miles. The formation passed BEAUVAIS Airfield where no aircraft were seen, but there were many unfilled bomb craters and damaged hangars. They crossed out at AULT at 8,000ft landing at base at 1805 hrs.

'COMBAT REPORT. 150 WING. W/CDR R.P. BEAMONT DSO DFC PILOT. 8 June 1944.

'I was leading the Newchurch Tempest Wing on a fighter sweep on the Caen area of the beachhead via Rouen, Bernay and Agentan. We took off from Newchurch at 12.25 hours, and crossed the French coast at Pte d'Ailly at 10,000ft. When we were a few miles to the West of Rouen at 12.50 hours over scattered cloud, I saw five aircraft in line astern at about 6,000ft, turning from East to North. Leaving 486 (N.Z.) Squadron up above as top cover, I took No 3 Squadron down to investigate.

'I closed in behind the aircraft at 470 I.A.S. and recognised them as Me 109Gs. They were travelling at approximately 300mph and did not realise they were being bounced until just before I had opened fire, when the e/a broke to port and dived for cloud with violent evasive action. I selected the fourth or last e/a, I am not sure which, and opened fire with a 2/3 second burst, starting with 30° deflection, and changing according to the e/a's evasive action.

'I opened fire at about 500 yards range closing to point blank, and saw strikes at the end of the burst on the starboard side of the fuselage. The e/a immediately poured smoke and flames. I had to break to starboard in order to avoid collision and then to port when I saw clearly the e/a enveloped in flames in an inverted dive. I broke to starboard as I finished my attack and heard a loud bang and saw a strike on my starboard wing. My No 2 who subsequently saw my e/a disintegrate and the starboard wing break off, saw two Me 109s diving down out of sun at him and myself. My u/c warning lights went on so I handed over to S/Ldr Dredge of No 3 Squadron, and set course for base where I landed at 13.30 hours.

'The aircraft I destroyed was camouflaged mottled chocolate and brown and no national markings were visible.

'I claim one Me 109G destroyed.

'Rounds fired: 60 rounds 20mm each gun H.E.I. and S.A.P.I. No stoppages.'

Appendix 9

'From: Air commodore C.A. Bouchier, C.B.E., D.F.C.

HEADQUARTERS NO. 11 GROUP,
ROYAL AIR FORCE
UXBRIDGE.
9th September, 1944.

Reference:
CAB/D.O.

'Dear Beamont,

'Air Marshal Sir Roderic Hill, K.C.B., M.C., A.F.C. has received a letter from Sir Ernest Gowers, K.C.B., K.B.E., London Regional Defence Commissioner, of which the following is an extract:-

"'At a recent meeting of my Standing Committee of Town Clerks of the London Region a spontaneous and unanimous request was made to me that I should convey to you, on behalf of the Local Authorities in the Region, their deep sense of obligation to the Pilots under your Command whose skill and devotion are doing so much to mitigate London's present ordeal. I gladly do this. We are filled with admiration of their magnificent achievements, and I hope you will find it possible to convey this tribute to them so that they may know how fully and gratefully London realises its debt to them."

'I feel the foregoing should be brought to the notice of all Wing Leaders, Squadron Commanders and Pilots concerned, not forgetting the splendid work also done by Control Staffs both at Sector and G.C.I. Stations.

'Yours sincerely,
C. Bouchier.

'Wing Commander R.P. Beamont, D.S.O., D.F.C.,
R.A.F. Station,
NEWCHURCH.'

Appendix 10

'*RAF Volkel (Holland) No 122 Wing 2nd Tactical Air Force Intelligence Bulletin*

'Tuesday 3rd October 1944

'Since the bulletin last appeared the Tempests have got thoroughly into their giant stride, having already destroyed 5 enemy aircraft, probably destroyed 2 and damaged 1 (since arriving in 2nd TAF on 24 September). . .

'On Sept 29th 96 sorties were flown for 118 hrs flying with 3 Fw 190s destroyed, 2 probables and 1 damaged; and one Tempest lost (F/O Clapperton missing). . .

'On Sept 30, 71 sorties produced 110 hrs flying with 1 Me 109 destroyed and F/O Rothwell (3 Sqdn) forcelanded, unhurt.

'On Oct 1st the squadrons. . .waited at Grimberghen until the mists lifted sufficiently to enable them to fly North (to Volkel). W/O Reid was shot down by flak on the way.

'Oct 2nd, 74 sorties flown totalling 79 hrs. Patrols of the Arnhem area uneventful except for the destruction of the Wing's 98th Hun since D Day, a Fw 190 destroyed by W/Cdr Beamont.

'*56 Squadron Report:*
'Monday 2nd October. VOLKEL.

'The squadron flew three patrols (Arnhem area). The first, led by S/Ldr Cotes Preedy was uneventful. W/Cdr Beamont led the second and 56 gained reflected glory as the W/Cdr Flying destroyed one Fw 190. This was a particularly fine piece of work as the flying was done, not in the horizontal but in the vertical plane, and the W/Cdr opened fire at 510 I.A.S. . . .'